D1562815

It's Only A Play

It's Only A Play

○ ○ ○ ○ ○ ○ ○ ○ ○ ○ ○ ○ ○

A Comedy by
TERRENCE McNALLY

Nelson Doubleday, Inc.
Garden City, New York

For Edgar Bronfman, Jr.

It's Only A Play was produced by the Manhattan Theatre Club at the Space, at City Center Theater opening on December 17, 1985. It was directed by John Tillinger with sets designed by John Lee Beatty, lighting designed by Pat Collins, costumes designed by Rita Ryack, sound designed by Stan Metelits and hairstyles by Brad Scott. The Production Stage Manager was Tracy B. Cohen.

GUS WASHINGTON	Jihmi Kennedy
JAMES WICKER	James Coco
VIRGINIA NOYES	Joanna Gleason
FRANK FINGER	David Garrison
JULIA BUDDER	Christine Baranski
IRA DREW	Paul Benedict
PETER AUSTIN	Mark Blum
EMMA	Florence Stanley

An earlier version of the play was produced by the Manhattan Punch Line opening on November 18, 1982.

It's Only A Play

The time of the play is now.

The place of the play is Julia Budder's town house.

The people of the play are

PETER AUSTIN	The playwright. Don't let his nice looks fool you.
JULIA BUDDER	The producer. Attractive and genuinely pleasant.
IRA DREW	The critic. Wears glasses. Very sure of himself.
FRANK FINGER	The director. Seething. Dark. Intense.
VIRGINIA NOYES	The star. High cheekbones. Throaty voice. A firecracker.
GUS WASHINGTON	The temporary help. Black, cool and street smart.
JAMES WICKER	The best friend. Pleasant, open features and a personality of great charm.
EMMA	A taxi driver. A no-nonsense lady of indeterminate years.

ACT ONE

○ ○ ○ ○ ○ ○ ○ ○ ○

ACT I

The bedroom in Julia Budder's town house. It is a large room with a king-sized bed, a chaise, several armchairs, a television set with a remote control, a bookcase, a desk with several telephones and, most curiously, a spinet piano.

There are two doors: one leads to the bathroom and dressing area, the other to the hallway and stairs. Thus, we can see people on the stairs before they enter the room itself. There are two windows, drapes drawn, fronting the street.

AT RISE: *There is a party in progress downstairs. Although the bedroom is empty, we can hear voices, laughter and piano music drifting up from the living room, one floor below. It sounds like a lot of people. Also, the bed is heaped with mink coats and purses.*

Gus Washington is seen coming up the stairs. He is dressed in a dinner jacket. He is carrying a load of mink coats. He comes into the bedroom and closes the door. The party sounds grow fainter.

He tosses the mink coats onto the pile and crosses to the desk, picks up the phone and excitedly punch-dials a number.

GUS: Hello, Homer? It's me again. Guess who just blew in down there this time? Lena Horne! Can you bear it? . . . The hell you say it isn't. I guess I know what Lena Horne looks like. It sure as shit ain't Leontyne Price. I'm telling you, Homer, this place is crawling with celebrities. The party of the year for the play of the season. There's one old dude down there talking to Shirley MacLaine I'm pretty sure is the Pope. If I'd've known it was gonna be this kind of a gig, I'd've brought my Instamatic. Homer, this could be my Golden Opportunity. I feel one mighty song coming on.

(James Wicker enters)

3

JAMES: *(To people offstage)* Wasn't it wonderful? I'll be right down. Thank you.

GUS: I seen this one somewhere too.

JAMES: Hello.

GUS: You looking for the bathroom? Across the hall.

JAMES: The telephone. I couldn't hear a thing down there.

GUS: I gotta go.

JAMES: That's perfectly all right.

GUS: It's all yours.

JAMES: Thank you. Hello? Hello?

GUS: Push the button.

JAMES: The button! Thank you. Hello, operator? This is Mr. Wicker again. Thank you. *(To Gus)* California. They're all dying to know how the play went tonight.

GUS: How did it go?

JAMES: Wonderful, just wonderful.

GUS: Mrs. Budder will be pleased. Too bad you're not a critic.

JAMES: We're all critics. You haven't seen the show?

GUS: I'm temporary help. This party is just a one-night stand for me.

JAMES: This party is a one-night stand for a lot of people.

4

GUS: I'm Gus, Gus Washington. See, I don't do this for a living. I'm a singer-slash-actor-slash-dancer-slash-comedian-slash-black belt karate expert-period.

JAMES: Oh. *(Into phone)* Hello? Hello?

GUS: I have studied acting in the Village with Norman Orland, of whom I guess you are familiar. If not, he studied with Evelyn Galyon, who was a man (did you ever hear of a man called Evelyn? Weird!). He's a wonderful teacher and I'd recommend him to you and anybody you might know.

JAMES: Thank you. *(Back into phone)* Yes, I'm still here, operator. Thank God you're back. Where else would I be? I didn't place this call. *(To Gus)* My agent calls me and I have to wait. She wouldn't do this to Don Johnson.

GUS: Ain't I seen you someplace?

JAMES: It's very likely.

GUS: Where?

JAMES: It all depends. The Broadway stage?

GUS: No.

JAMES: Motion pictures, maybe?

GUS: No.

JAMES: Then, it must be television.

GUS: No.

JAMES: No? What do you mean, no?

GUS: Maybe I saw you walking your dog.

5

JAMES: I don't have a dog. Besides, I live in Beverly Hills. I have a series.

GUS: Yeah?

JAMES: "Out on a Limb."

GUS: "Out on a Limb"? Is that you in that show?

JAMES: I'm afraid so.

GUS: I've watched that program.

JAMES: I'm glad you don't have a Nielsen box. *(Into phone)* Hello? There you are! Finally! What? I can hardly hear you. Whose party are you at? Does he know his series has been canceled? Give him my love. "How did it go tonight?" Wonderful, just wonderful. *(He covers the phone and holds his empty champagne glass toward Gus)* Gus? Would you mind terribly?

GUS: Some more of the bubbly, right?

JAMES: And close the door on your way out. *(Torch is heard in the bathroom, a terrible sound to behold)* What in God's name is that?

GUS: The dog.

JAMES: What dog?

GUS: The Budders' dog. They call him Torch. Ain't nobody supposed to let him out. He got out when the party first started and bit that woman who was on "What's My Line."

JAMES: Not Arlene Francis?

GUS: That's the one.

6

JAMES: Torch bit Arlene Francis?

GUS: Went right for her face.

JAMES: How horrible! I'm supposed to do her show next week.

GUS: They took her to Mount Sinai along with Mr. Budder.

JAMES: *(Into phone)* Hold on, darling, this is too good. *(To Gus)* What happened to Mr. Budder?

GUS: He got mugged right after the play tonight.

JAMES: Where was he? Eighth Avenue, trying to get a cab?

GUS: The men's room in Sardi's, taking a leak.

(Gus goes)

JAMES: *(Into phone)* I'm sitting ten feet from a rabid dog who just bit Arlene Francis in the town house of a lady producer whose husband got mugged in the men's room at Sardi's. I will never knock California again. Where was I? Oh, the play! *(He makes himself comfortable for a long haul on the telephone. His voice glows with relish)* Darling, what is your traditional Thanksgiving dinner? . . . Well, this one is a thirty-five-pound Butterball. Bob Fosse asked me what I thought at intermission and all I said was "Gobble, gobble" and he wet himself. Of course I don't want you to give that to Liz Smith. Are you crazy? I may want to work with these people. How was Jack Nimble? He was terrible, just terrible. But tell me this and tell me no more: when was he ever any good? All of my mannerisms and none of my warmth. Of course I would have been wonderful in it. It was written for me. And you want to hear the killer? I wasn't even mentioned in Peter's biography in the *Playbill*. I mean, let's face it. I did create the lead in his one and only hit, but do you think I got so much as even a mention in his bio tonight? Well, that's a best friend for you. I fly in three thousand miles on the goddamn Red Eye for his opening and I'm not even mentioned in the goddamn *Playbill*. The egos in this business! What about Virginia Noyes? Terrible, just terrible. I haven't seen a performance like that since her last one. Well, of course she wanted to come back to Broadway. After her last couple of pictures, she had to go somewhere. Terrible direction, just terrible. Boy wonder he may well be; the new Trevor Nunn he's not. He's not even the old Mike Nichols. Frank something. He's out of Chicago. Aren't they all? Sets? What sets? It took place on a goddamn tilted disk. Give me scenery or count me out. Hideous costumes. Darling, I would have made my first entrance in a leather codpiece and sort of antlers. I kid you not. There but for the grace of ABC went I! Darling, Arnold Schwarzenegger couldn't have held this one up. Oh, and guess who was sitting next to me at the theater? Rita Moreno in a Day-Glo turban. She was with Calvin Klein. I wish you could have seen her face when he introduced her to Jean Kennedy as Chita Rivera! Who? Rita or Chita? Terrible, just terrible. But listen, darling, what do I know? What do any of us old gypsies know? I liked *The Rink*.

(Virginia Noyes enters the bedroom)

VIRGINIA: Is there a can in here? That fucking Shirley MacLaine's had me in a corner telling me who she was in her previous lives until I thought I would burst.

JAMES: You were wonderful tonight, just wonderful. I'm just telling the Coast.

VIRGINIA: You got the Coast on there? Give me that mother. *(She takes the receiver)* Hey, California. This is Virginia Noyes. I'm back on Broadway, feeling fabulous, and you can all go fuck yourself! *(Hands phone back to James)* Am I going to regret that?

JAMES: Only if you're going back to California.

VIRGINIA: After tonight? No way! *(She exits into bathroom)*

JAMES: Oh my God! Miss Noyes, Miss Noyes!

VIRGINIA: What do you want? I just got in here!

JAMES: Be careful of that dog in there.

VIRGINIA: What dog?

JAMES: There's a dog in there with you.

VIRGINIA: Is that what that is? *(Laughs)*

JAMES: *(Into phone)* Virginia Noyes, looking like Pocahontas and feeling no pain. Washed up at thirty-seven, that's the tragedy . . . Thirty-seven, darling, I know these things. Listen, what were our ratings like this week? . . . That's not good. *(Gus returns with a bottle of champagne)* I don't like that, Sue, I don't like that at all. I told them not to put us in that time slot. *(To Gus, who leaves)* Thank you, Gus. *(Back into phone)* I can't compete with trained dolphins. Cagney & Lacey I can handle, but I draw the line at fish. They can't cancel us. I'll kill myself. Tell ABC I'll kill myself. Besides, I'm having a tennis court moved. Don't they know what that costs? Please, Sue, I don't need stress. I'm here to celebrate the opening of my best friend's play. I'll be back late tomorrow. We'll schmooze. Yes, mother. Yes, yes, yes. Big kisses. Ciao. *(He hangs up. Gus enters, struggling with a fur coat of exaggerated length)* Don't tell me. Let me guess. Tommy Tune, right?

GUS: I just take coats. I don't ask names. Mrs. Budder just got back from the hospital.

JAMES: Where is she, the dear?

GUS: She'll be right up. She wants you to wait for her.

JAMES: Up here? What for? I'm missing everything.

9

GUS: She didn't say.

JAMES: I want to go to the party.

(Virginia comes out of the bathroom)

VIRGINIA: You know, there is a dog in there when you get right up close to it.

JAMES: What did you think it was?

VIRGINIA: My first husband.

GUS: You let somebody in there?

VIRGINIA: I hope you guys are cool. *(She has already sat with her drug stash)* It's straight city down there. My agent said, "Ginny, don't let anyone see you doing that. You're not in Hollywood. That's Helen Hayes over there." I said, "Honey, I don't give a flying fuck if it's Gabby Hayes. I am going to get a little buzz on."

GUS: You got some stuff there, lady?

VIRGINIA: I got some of everything. Grass, Thai stick, hash, coke, ludes, uppers, downers, saccharine, this stuff'll kill you, Vitamin E, Revlon Lip Gloss, Tiger Balm. *(To James)* You want a hit?

JAMES: No, thank you. I had some at home.

VIRGINIA: *(To Gus)* You?

GUS: No, thank you, I gotta stay on the ball. Maybe I'll catch you later. *(He goes)*

VIRGINIA: He's kinda cute.

10

JAMES: He didn't have a clue who I was and he wants to be an actor!

VIRGINIA: Who are you?

JAMES: I'm James Wicker.

VIRGINIA: Right.

JAMES: We did a film together.

VIRGINIA: Which one?

JAMES: *Red Dawn.*

VIRGINIA: Was I in that? I'm sure it'll come back. Did you ever have more hair?

JAMES: No, that was Marlo Thomas. We're often mistaken.

VIRGINIA: I'm sorry. James Wicker! Of course! How could I forget? *Flashes,* Peter's first play. He really put you on the map with that one.

JAMES: Some people would say it's the other way around.

VIRGINIA: Hello again. I love your work. I love it, I love it.

JAMES: Thank you.

VIRGINIA: When I forget someone, I really forget someone. How the hell are you? You look marvelous.

JAMES: I came in on the Red Eye.

VIRGINIA: When they sent me Peter's play, they told me you were doing Jack's part.

11

JAMES: There was some talk about it, they wanted me desperately, as a matter of fact, but with my series . . .

VIRGINIA: You got a series?

JAMES: For five years now.

VIRGINIA: I'm sorry. I do a lot of self-destructive things, but I draw the line at television. I don't watch it and I won't do it.

JAMES: I just take the money and run.

VIRGINIA: Yeah. But are you happy?

JAMES: Relatively. Are you?

VIRGINIA: Fan-fucking-tastic.

JAMES: Speaking of Peter.

VIRGINIA: Peter? I wrote the book. Oh, that Peter!

JAMES: Where is he?

VIRGINIA: Beats me. Maybe he's just hiding until the reviews are out. Speaking of which, have you heard anything?

JAMES: You're home free with this one.

VIRGINIA: You really think so?

JAMES: Darling, I could phone these raves in.

VIRGINIA: I hope so. Living in L.A. so long, you forget what being on a real stage is like. My only mistake was going out there in the first place. I guess I just wanted to see myself forty feet tall.

JAMES: We all do.

VIRGINIA: I wanted to see what they'd do with my tits.

JAMES: Me too.

VIRGINIA: I don't see the crime in that.

JAMES: It's the American Dream.

VIRGINIA: I see the asshole but I don't see the crime. Thank God for this play. Don't you miss all this?

JAMES: No way. Wild horses couldn't get me up there again.

VIRGINIA: *(Standing)* I don't know about you, but my loins are girded.

JAMES: I'd love to but I'm waiting for our hostess. If Mary Martin sings, I'll come down.

VIRGINIA: If Carol Channing sings, I'll come up!

(Virginia goes; James looks at his watch)

JAMES: It must be getting time for the first reviews. *(He turns on the television with remote-control module)* Oh, God, I dread this. They're gonna crucify him.

(Frank Finger comes into the bedroom)

FRANK: *(To people offstage)* I don't wanna hear. I don't wanna know. *(To James)* Hi.

JAMES: Hi! I'm James Wicker. Do you know who's reviewing for Channel 5 now?

FRANK: No. Do you have to have that thing on? Reviews are killing the theater.

JAMES: Good ones aren't.

13

FRANK: *(He is holding up a small enamel box)* How much do you think something like this is worth?

JAMES: I don't know. Several hundred dollars, I should think. It used to be . . . what was his name? He gave me that incredible rave.

FRANK: You an actor?

JAMES: Yes.

FRANK: New York?

JAMES: Ex. L.A.

FRANK: L.A. sucks. Several hundred dollars for a box?

JAMES: It's more than just a box. It's an antique box.

FRANK: Puh! *(He pockets the box. James's eyes widen in disbelief. Frank looks right at him)* What?

JAMES: I saw that.

FRANK: So?

JAMES: I . . . *(For once, he is speechless)*

FRANK: What's upstairs?

JAMES: I don't know. More rooms, I should think. Whoever you are, you're putting me in an extremely difficult position. *(Frank presses remote television control. The sound comes up at once)*

TV: Stewart Klein was at the Barrymore Theatre for the opening of a new play tonight.

14

JAMES: I would like to be able to enjoy this. *(The lure of the first review is too much for him. He rushes for a seat in front of the television)*

STEWART KLEIN'S VOICE: Well, it's like this. Peter Austin's eagerly awaited new play, *The Golden Egg*, love that title, is—

(Frank presses the remote again. The sound goes off)

JAMES: What happened?

FRANK: You don't want to watch that.

JAMES: The hell I don't.

(Frank turns the sound back up for a second)

STEWART KLEIN'S VOICE: . . . working in an idiom totally dissimilar from his previous plays, almost as if they were in preparation for this, his Broadway debut, Mr. Austin has given us a play that is both—

(Frank turns the sound off. This time, James spins around)

FRANK: Watching only encourages them.

JAMES: What's the matter with you? Are you crazy? Now, turn that set on.

FRANK: I'd rather know what you thought.

JAMES: I loved it. And now I'd like to know what he thought.

FRANK: What do you care?

JAMES: He's a critic.

FRANK: He's an asshole.

15

JAMES: That's not the point.

FRANK: What is the point?

JAMES: What the assholes think.

FRANK: I'd rather know what you thought.

JAMES: I told you. I loved it. Please. *(He has fallen to his knees. The reviews of Peter's play are a matter of life and death to James)*

FRANK: Why?

JAMES: Because my best friend wrote it. What do you want from me?

FRANK: A better reason.

JAMES: All right. My best friend wrote it for me and I turned it down because I thought it was a piece of shit and I want to see if that asshole agrees with me.

FRANK: Your best friend?

JAMES: Peter. Peter Austin.

FRANK: Peter Austin wrote a piece of shit for you?

JAMES: Not on purpose. In this business, we're all capable of shit.

(Frank turns up the volume)

STEWART KLEIN'S VOICE: . . . superb, no, I take that back: perfect staging by Frank Finger, the brilliant young director who gave us last season's ravishing *Arden of Feversham* in Prospect Park. Thank you and good night.

(There is a burst of applause from the party downstairs)

TV ANNOUNCER: That was Stewart Klein with the very first review of tonight's big opening at the Ethel Barrymore. I'll be right back with Ticho Parley and the sports.

(Frank turns off TV with remote control. There is an enormous cheer and another burst of applause from the party downstairs)

JAMES: He liked it? He must have liked it!

FRANK: Why not? Look who directed it.

JAMES: Please, don't give me Frank Finger. You're talking to someone who actually sat through his all-male *Wild Duck.*

FRANK: I'm Frank Finger.

JAMES: And it was wonderful, just wonderful. So you're Frank Finger.

(The bedroom door opens. Julia Budder is seen on the landing calling over her shoulder to some guests on the floor below)

JULIA: Thank you! Isn't it exciting? I won't be a moment.

FRANK: *(Tossing the purloined antique box to James)* I'll tell Peter what you thought of his play.

JAMES: I'll deny every word of it.

(Julia comes into the bedroom just as Frank is on his way out)

JULIA: Congratulations, Frank.

FRANK: I don't want to hear! I don't want to know! *(Frank is gone)*

JAMES: There she is!

17

JULIA: I'm sorry.

JAMES: Congratulations, darling. How does it feel to have the biggest hit on Broadway since *Virginia Woolf?*

JULIA: You really think so?

JAMES: Not only is Julia Budder the luckiest producer on Broadway, she's also the prettiest.

JULIA: I have never been so embarrassed in my entire life.

JAMES: What happened?

JULIA: This! *(She raises her skirt to reveal a pair of men's galoshes under her evening gown)* I've had them on all evening. I was so excited, I completely forgot.

JAMES: So what! Darling, this is your night. You can take the dress off and keep the boots on. It's opening night, anything goes. You can do, say or feel anything you want. *(He will quickly be sorry he said this. Julia lets out a scream. Actually, it is more of a happy squeal. She even twirls herself around a time or two. James looks at her with some amazement and much impatience)*

JULIA: I did it. I did it. I did it. I'm a real live Broadway producer. You really think we have a chance?

JAMES: *(Sticking out his hand)* Dinner at Lutèce.

JULIA: *(Without a moment's hesitation)* You're on. *(She shakes his hand)* You heard Stewart Kling?

JAMES: Stewart Kling?

JULIA: He reviews for Channel 11 or 9 or . . . he was just on.

JAMES: Stewart Klein, Channel 5.

18

JULIA: That's him. You didn't watch?

JAMES: Thanks to your director.

JULIA: *(Taking off her mink coat)* Frank just has a phobia about reviews. I don't know why. His are always good. *(Shaking her head at it all)* Irving Berlin said it best: "There's no business like the one we're in."

JAMES: What did he say?

JULIA: "There's no business like—"

JAMES: Stewart Klein.

JULIA: I'll never forget it. My first review. It's engraved right here in great big letters. "Good, solid theater."

JAMES: "Good, solid theater"?

JULIA: You have to imagine it blown up.

JAMES: "Good, solid theater."

JULIA: To tell you the truth, I was hoping for something with a little more oomph in it myself, but coming from him our press agent says it's a rave.

JAMES: Who's your press agent?

JULIA: Buzz, Buzz something. *(Heading for bathroom)*

JAMES: Buzz something?

JULIA: He's tops in his field. Hello, Torch. Mummy's home, darling. We were a bad boy tonight. James, would you bring me Torch's Yummies? They're in the silver dish on the coffee table. *(She goes back into the bathroom. A strong reaction from James, who had been unknowingly eating Torch's Yum-*

19

*mies throughout his telephone conversation with the Coast.
James brings Julia the Yummies, then pours himself another
glass of champagne as Julia comes out of the bathroom)*

JAMES: Gus said you wanted to speak to me?

JULIA: Just let me collect myself. The hospital was a nightmare.

JAMES: So he told me. What happened, exactly?

JULIA: Well, first Elliott gets mugged in the men's room at Sardi's. No one gets mugged in the men's room at Sardi's. It's never happened in their entire history and they're not a new restaurant. Thank God, they caught him.

JAMES: Who was it?

JULIA: Just some radical busboy. And then Torch bites Arlene Francis and it's off to Mount Sinai with *her.* I said to her, "Relax, Arlene, he just wants to sniff you." People don't know how to behave around dogs; horses either, for that matter. I'm not budging from this house again tonight. Have you seen that mob down there? *(She has caught her breath by now)*

JAMES: No, but I'd like to.

JULIA: I don't know half of them. I think I saw Candice Bergen in the library. I used to listen to her father. I'm sure she did too. I said to one woman, "Excuse me, you look just like Marilyn Horne." She said, "I am Marilyn Horne."

JAMES: Oh, Jackie's here? Come on, I'll introduce you.

JULIA: I hate to do this to you, but I'm very worried about Peter.

JAMES: What's wrong?

JULIA: This. *(She produces a sealed envelope)* Just before the play tonight, I was backstage with the actors, giving them their ashtrays, when the stage manager handed me this note.

JAMES: May I?

JULIA: I had to promise not to read it until after the reviews were in.

JAMES: And so you opened it at once?

JULIA: Of course not. But now that there's no sign of him, I'll never forgive myself if anything happens to him.

JAMES: *(His hand out for the note)* Julia.

JULIA: But James, I promised.

JAMES: I didn't. *(He takes the note and tears it open)*

JULIA: If it's bad news, I don't want to hear it.

JAMES: *(Reading rather quickly; the party still beckons)* "Dear Julia. Thank you for producing my play. I know it cost you a lot of money, none of which you may ever see again."

JULIA: The money! As if I cared about that.

JAMES: "And thank you for your beautiful opening-night gift. I have always wanted a handmade ashtray with the name of one of my plays on it."

JULIA: I had Little Elliott make everyone in the cast an ashtray with the name of the play and opening date on it.

JAMES: Little Elliott?

JULIA: Our eight-year-old.

21

JAMES: I think Peter's being sarcastic.

JULIA: Oh, no, they're really quite lovely. Look.

(James looks at it a beat, then resumes with the letter)

JAMES: "I wish you the best. I even wish Frank break a leg."

JULIA: That's a theatrical expression. It means good luck.

JAMES: What does he mean, "even"?

JULIA: You should've heard some of the names Frank called him during rehearsal. Failure. Has-been. Hack.

JAMES: No!

JULIA: Loser. Fake. Phony. Written out.

JAMES: I get the picture.

JULIA: He said I was just an amateur, dilettante, rich bitch.

JAMES: Why did you stand for it?

JULIA: I didn't. My husband said, "You can't speak to my wife like that," and he punched him right in the mouth.

JAMES: Good for Elliott.

JULIA: You don't understand. Frank punched Elliott. He knocked him out and then barred him from the theater.

JAMES: As the producer, you should have done something.

JULIA: I'd already been barred from the theater.

JAMES: This play sounds like a total nightmare for you from the first day of rehearsal right up until tonight.

JULIA: It's been bliss. Sheer creative bliss.

JAMES: "As for me, my dearest Julia (and I love you like a mother)"—

JULIA: And I love him like a son.

JAMES: "I don't think I can face anyone, most of all you, if I let us down tonight. If anything happens to me, it will be an accident and you are in no major way to blame."

JULIA: *(A knife cutting through her)* Major!

JAMES: "Good-bye for now. Remember me a little bit. And good luck with the Lanford Wilson."

JULIA: A new play I've optioned.

JAMES: "P.S. I still wish you'd given me that turntable in the second act." *(He looks up)* For this we're missing the party of the year?

JULIA: Where *is* he, then?

JAMES: Darling, Peter is a genius at theatrics. You've heard of a late entrance? It's an old stunt. Believe me, I do it all the time.

JULIA: I hope you're right. *(Gus has entered with a pile of coats)* There you are, Fred.

GUS: It's Gus.

JULIA: I'm sorry. Gus. Who do all those coats belong to?

GUS: *La Cage aux Folles.*

JULIA: I don't remember inviting *La Cage aux Folles.*

GUS: Everybody's asking for you down there.

23

JULIA: We're just on our way down. *(Calling to James)* James? *(But now it's James who is transfixed. He is reading the other side of Peter's note)*

GUS: They're all saying you've got a big, big hit, Mrs. Budder.

JULIA: From your lips to God's ears. Thank you, Gus. *(Gus goes)* James?

JAMES: "P.S. The play never really had a chance without James Wicker in it. Of course, he was a son of a bitch not to have done it and I wish him and his fucking series a sudden and violent death. No hard feelings, Jim, you miserable, no-talent fruit, but you will rot in hell for this. P.P.S. Believe it or not, I love you. The Nipper."

(There is a pause)

JULIA: You call him The Nipper?

JAMES: Just a nickname I had for him.

JULIA: Had?

JAMES: Have, have!

JULIA: I'm sure he doesn't mean that side of the note either.

JAMES: "No hard feelings, you miserable, no-talent fruit."

JULIA: You? No-talent? That's ridiculous.

JAMES: You certainly came off a hell of a lot better than I did.

(Gus enters with coats; Julia takes galoshes and bag into bathroom)

GUS: They're having the time of their lives down there. Lena Horne just finished singing "Stormy Weather," and Beverly

Sills burst into something from *Faust*. I was hoping maybe I could sing something tonight.

JULIA: Sing, dear? Sing what?

GUS: A song. You know, audition.

JULIA: I don't see why not. *(To James)* I'll only be a moment.

JAMES: Julia!

JULIA: I only use Equity members when I entertain. I believe we of the theater should extend a helping hand whenever we can. *(She is heading toward the piano)* What are you going to sing for us, Gus?

GUS: "Raindrops Keep Falling Upon My Head."

JULIA: One of my favorites. What key? *(Seating herself at the piano, she flashes Gus her most radiant smile and gives him a tonic chord for his song. He has a big, booming voice. After a moment or two of this torture, James gets to his feet. The phone starts ringing)* My very most private number. It could only be Elliott. I won't be a moment. *(She goes to the phone. Gus continues to sing, turning all his attention to James now)* Darling, how are you? . . .

JAMES: *(To Gus as he ushers him out of the room)* Wonderful, just wonderful. *(Toward phone)* Your wife's got a big fat hit on her hands, Elliott!

JULIA: *(Into phone)* Jimmy Wicker. Darling, I've been talking to Howard and he thinks we should pull out of the resort in Santo Domingo while we're ahead and consider those condominiums in Nova Scotia . . . Mmmmmmm . . . Mmmmmmm . . . Mmmmmmm.

(James has started browsing through a pile of play scripts that are stacked on a coffee table in front of him)

JAMES: *(Reading aloud) Bluestocking,* by Caroline Comstock. *(Ira Drew comes into the bedroom. He has a furtive air. There are dandruff flakes on the lapel of his ill-fitting tuxedo)* At rise: nothing. Ten seconds of this.

JULIA: That's exactly what I told him.

JAMES: The lights come up on a green chair. It is empty. A woman screams in the distance. [Or is it a woman?] We hear a flourish of wind. [Or is it wind?]

(Ira leans over James)

IRA: How do you like it so far? *(James jumps at the intrusion)* I'm sorry. I'm waiting for Mrs. Budder.

JAMES: I'm afraid this room's off limits.

IRA: I just need a quick word with her. *(He gestures toward James)* And talk about killing two birds with one stone!

JAMES: I beg your pardon?

IRA: I gave you a wonderful notice once.

JAMES: You did?

IRA: That little Lorca play at the Theatre DeLys, remember?

JAMES: No, that was Gordon Small.

IRA: Gordon Small, of course. Wonderful actor.

JAMES: Wasn't he?

IRA: Wasn't? What do you mean, wasn't?

26

JAMES: Is. I meant is. At least I assume he's still around. Gordon hasn't worked much lately. Ever since the Theatre DeLys, in fact.

IRA: *Uncle Vanya* in Chicago?

JAMES: No, I don't think . . .

IRA: James Wacker, of course. *(Remembering his quote)* "James Wacker is a consummate actor. His Mercutio was a pip." I never forget what I write about anyone.

JAMES: Wicker.

IRA: Hmm?

JAMES: James Wicker.

IRA: I know that.

JAMES: You said Wacker.

IRA: No! *(Starting to laugh)* Wacker! *(It's growing)* That's terrible. *(It's out of control already)* Wacker!

JAMES: And you are?

IRA: I'm sorry. I just assumed. Ira Drew.

JAMES: *The* Ira Drew?

IRA: There's another?

(James offers some Yummies to Ira)

JULIA: Darling, this isn't going to affect our trip. Let me write it down or I'll forget. Golf clubs.

JAMES: Wasn't the play wonderful tonight?

IRA: You'll have to wait two weeks to find out what I thought *and* it'll cost you two-fifty.

JAMES: Two-fifty for a magazine!

IRA: Thirty-five dollars for an orchestra seat.

JAMES: *(Absolving himself)* I'm on television now. I'm free. Besides, critics don't pay for their tickets.

IRA: This one does. The League of Producers barred me from the press list. "Too vicious." I call them as I see them.

JAMES: You've always been very good to me.

IRA: Television? I wondered what happened to you.

JULIA: *(The house phone is buzzing her)* They're calling me from downstairs. I'll have to get back to you . . .

JAMES: Her husband.

IRA: He invented toilet paper?

JAMES: Perfected it. Rich as Croesus.

IRA: I can see why.

JULIA: *(Still on the phone)* I love you, too. Stop, you're making me blush . . . I said stop, you're making me blush! *(She hangs up)* That man! *(It's clear she adores him)*

IRA: This is Ira Drew, Julia.

JULIA: *(Brightly)* Hello!

JAMES: *The* Ira Drew.

28

JULIA: *(A merry laugh)* There's another? *(Into the house phone)* No, I didn't invite the cast of *Annie*. Tell them to go away. I'm sorry, but they can't come in. *(She hangs up)* More crashers. I'm sorry, Mr. Drew.

IRA: I'll come right to the point. I really shouldn't be up here with you at all.

JAMES: Excuse me, Julia, I'll be downstairs.

IRA: Please, stay. This concerns the both of you. You've been sent a new play to consider, Mrs. Budder, a certain *Bluestocking*.

JULIA: Yes, I have. It came this morning.

JAMES: I was just leafing through it.

IRA: *Bluestocking* is the best American play I've come across in a long time. It has humor, depth, wit, wisdom, compassion, truth, a small cast and one set.

JULIA: It sounds like a producer's dream.

JAMES: Next thing you'll be telling us is you wrote it.

IRA: Caroline Comstock wrote *Bluestocking!* We've all heard the same sordid rumors about our relationship. I can't help them. But Caroline is only my protégée, nothing less and nothing more. I'm merely Svengali to her Trilby, Pygmalion to her Galatea, John Derek to her Bo.

JULIA: Why are you telling us this?

IRA: We need new faces in the theater. New voices, new visions. Caroline's day will come, Mrs. Budder. I'd like to see yours come with her.

29

JULIA: Thank you, but for tonight I'm concentrating on Peter Austin's day.

IRA: You haven't much time. Even as we speak, the Shuberts are dickering for an option. David Merrick is— *(He turns suddenly as Gus enters with a new pile of coats)*

GUS: *Cats* and *42nd Street* are here. *(Ira makes a "Sssshh" motion. They all look at Gus. He dumps the coats on the bed. They continue to look at him)* Don't pay me no mind, Miss Scarlett! *(He goes)*

IRA: Can he be trusted?

JULIA: He's bonded, if that means anything.

IRA: No one must ever know of this meeting. It is highly unethical. Like a weekend in the Hamptons together, it would compromise the three of us.

JAMES: What did I do?

IRA: *Bluestocking* was written for you, Mr. Wicker.

JAMES: Two minutes ago you wondered what had happened to me.

IRA: Wait'll I tell Miss Comstock I've found you. I place my reputation in your hands. *(He is bowing out backwards)*

IRA: Thank you for your consideration, Mrs. Budder.

JULIA: Thank you for your inside lead, Mr. Drew.

JAMES: I'm always looking for the right vehicle!

IRA: It awaits you! *(He is gone, falling downstairs)*

JULIA: Mr. Drew, are you alright?

IRA: *(Offstage)* Fine.

JAMES: Certainly he's the last person I would have expected to see here tonight.

JULIA: I didn't invite him. He came with Lina Wertmüller.

JAMES: That's a fun couple! *(He puts down the play script)* "The American theatre would be a better place today if Peter Austin's parents had smothered him in his crib."

JULIA: What a horrible thing to say!

JAMES: Ira Drew's review of *Flashes.* I just hope he doesn't run into Peter down there.

(Peter Austin runs into the bedroom. He is in evening tails and outer coat. Gus is in pursuit.)

JULIA: It's all right, Gus.

GUS: He ran right by me.

JULIA: It's The Nipper.

GUS: Who?

JULIA: Mr. Austin wrote *The Golden Egg.*

GUS: Well, why didn't he say so? Gus. Gus Washington, actor. *(He goes)*

PETER: I just hope the next young American playwright who has a play open on Broadway doesn't have the misfortune of walking into his opening-night party with Arthur Miller right behind him.

JULIA: Peter, what happened?

31

PETER: All my life I dreamed they'd yell "Author, author!" when I got there. Instead what I got was "Arthur, Arthur!" He just won another Nobel Prize or something.

JAMES: Hello, Judas.

PETER: Is that who I think it is? You made it. You actually came.

JAMES: I wouldn't have missed this for anything.

PETER: Do you know who this is, Julia?

JULIA: Well, of course I do.

JAMES: Then, you're the first one this evening who does.

PETER: I love this man. I don't care who knows it. I love this person.

JAMES: Even though you wish him and his television series—.

JULIA: James!

PETER: Maybe I can get through all this now. This means everything. Thanks, Jimmy. *(He hugs him)*

JULIA: I wish I had my camera!

PETER: You look marvelous.

JAMES: Thank you.

PETER: Guess how many times I threw up today?

JULIA: I couldn't.

PETER: Actually leaned over the bowl and heaved my guts up?

JULIA: Is this a game?

PETER: Seven. Seven whole times. That's what this night means to me. Well ask James, Jimmy, Jim, Jimbo.

JAMES: Just be careful. This is a new tux.

PETER: Where are you staying?

JAMES: The Sherry.

JULIA: Peter, you had us all so worried. Where have you been?

PETER: You promise not to laugh?

JULIA: Of course not.

PETER: I've been out there growing up.

JULIA: I'm going to cry.

PETER: No, I mean it.

JULIA: So do I. That's wonderful.

PETER: You know where I spent our opening? In that bar across the street.

JULIA: I didn't know there was a bar across the street.

PETER: From the theater.

JULIA: For a moment . . ! My heart!

PETER: It felt like I'd written the longest first act in theater history.

JAMES: I know.

PETER: Thank God for Dolores Guber. She was in the original production of *Panama Hattie*. I told her I had a play opening.

33

That play. "Welcome to the theater, kid," she said. I told her I was already in the theater. You know, off-Broadway, off-off. "They ain't theater," she said and nodded towards the Barrymore, "That's theater." And then it was intermission. I saw you, Jimmy, talking to Bob Fosse. He was bent over double. God, you are a funny man. I wanted to cross the street and join you. Instead I threw up. I walked over to St. Patrick's, but it was closed, so I just walked around the theater district. So many theaters dark. Marquees left up because nothing new has come in. It's scary. I felt such a responsibility. I saw that goddamn new hotel.

JAMES: Terrible, just terrible.

PETER: They tore down three theaters for that? *Streetcar* opened at the same theater we did tonight. December 3, 1947. My birthday. How could you tear that down? By now it was after the play and everyone was gone. Our marquee was still lit. I think that was the first time I really saw it. Before that I was always too nervous. *The Golden Egg*, a new play by Peter Austin. It's a beautiful marquee, Julia. Downtown we never had that. Don't believe anyone who says it isn't nice. And then someone inside turned the lights off and we went dark. It was like we never existed. It's only a play. I grabbed the first cab I saw; it was a lulu! and asked them to drop me off here, then go to the *Times* and wait for the review. This is where I want to be and the people I most want to be with, if not for the rest of my life, at least until the *Times* is out.

JULIA: Next play I promise you that turntable.

PETER: Next play I'm going to want two turntables.

JULIA: Done! That's the Peter I like to see.

JAMES: Are you grown up? Can we go down now?

JULIA: James . . !

JAMES: I cry at a red hat.

PETER: I wanted you up there so bad tonight.

JAMES: Jack's marvelous.

PETER: I know.

JAMES: Not that marvelous.

PETER: They're already talking about Redford for the film.

JAMES: What of? *(Julia is tiptoeing toward the bathroom)*

JAMES: Julia!

JULIA: I won't be a moment. *(She makes "reconciliation" gestures to James. Peter doesn't see them)*

PETER: I guess I have to go down there and take my bows.

JAMES: You deserve them. It's quite a party. It looks like all Broadway is down there.

PETER: What's left of it.

JAMES: The opening night of *Flashes* we were taking bows in that Spanish restaurant on Bleecker Street. What was it called?

PETER: I got so drunk. It's a video rental shop now.

JAMES: The Jai Alai Restaurant.

PETER: Opening night of *Flashes* really was more about you than me.

JAMES: The first hysteria, maybe. It put us both on the map.

35

PETER: I wish it could have been the two of us again tonight.

JAMES: So do I. Peter, I wish you the best possible success with this play.

PETER: You really liked it?

JAMES: Peter, I'm the last one to ask. I was a middle-aged, not-Robert-Redford-looking character actor, one of thousands in this city. I would have gone on having ten lines in each act in New York and forty lines in stock for the rest of my life. Maybe once, just once, I would have played Willy Loman or Falstaff in a city my friends and my agent wouldn't mind coming to. And I would have gone on thinking I was lucky. Then you sent me *Flashes*. Make no mistake: I knew I was very, very lucky.

PETER: Then, I'm very glad I saw you do those ten lines in that awful play at the Cherry Lane.

JAMES: So am I. And it was fourteen lines. I was on a roll that season.

PETER: Jack was okay tonight?

JAMES: Jack was fine.

PETER: Now he was just "fine"!

(Julia opens the bathroom door)

JULIA: May I come out?

PETER: May we go down?

JAMES: Does anybody remember what food tastes like?

(Virginia opens the door to the bedroom and comes in)

36

Christine Baranski, Jihmi Kennedy and James Coco

Joanna Gleason, David Garrison, Mark Blum and James Coco

Mark Blum and Paul Benedict

David Garrison and Joanna Gleason

James Coco, Florence Stanley and Mark Blum

VIRGINIA: There you are! Where the fuck have you been? All my friends want to meet you.

PETER: Look at that *faccia*. Is this a star or is this a star?

VIRGINIA: Was I good tonight?

PETER: You're always good. Tonight you were fantastic.

VIRGINIA: I didn't want to let you down.

PETER: You didn't. Other than . . .

VIRGINIA: What?

PETER: Nothing.

VIRGINIA: Tell me.

PETER: It's so small.

JULIA: When she dropped the bottle?

VIRGINIA: I didn't drop the fucking bottle. It fucking slipped. What?

PETER: You know that line in the second act?

VIRGINIA: What line?

PETER: Where you're supposed to say, "It's about time," to Jack when he enters in the second scene.

VIRGINIA: It's one of my highlights. What's the matter? I said it, didn't I?

PETER: You said, "There you are."

VIRGINIA: So?

37

PETER: Instead of "It's about time." But no matter, no matter. I don't even know why I mentioned it. It's only a line.

VIRGINIA: So bring me up on Equity charges.

PETER: You asked me.

VIRGINIA: Please, I insist.

PETER: I'm sorry.

VIRGINIA: Playwrights!

PETER: Actors!

JULIA: The theater!

PETER: Is word perfect asking so much, Lord?

JAMES: Is a little nourishment?

VIRGINIA: I'm sorry, Peter, tomorrow night it'll be "There you are."

PETER: "It's about time"!

(Peter and Virginia hug)

VIRGINIA: It doesn't get any better than this!

PETER: I hope not!

VIRGINIA: Hey, quit shaking!

PETER: An evening like this is every playwright's rite of passage. Look to your laurels, Mr. Miller, here comes the next generation!

JULIA: Bravo! Bravo!

(Peter and Virginia exit the bedroom)

JAMES: As Bette Davis once said, "Who do you have to fuck to get something to eat around here?"

JULIA: Me, darling!

(Julia and James make ready to leave the bedroom as Frank comes into the room)

FRANK: I should have played poker in Tribeca with Robert Wilson and Pina Bausch. If one more person tells me I am a genius I am going to freak out.

JULIA: But you are a genius, darling.

FRANK: I am not.

JULIA: I'm sorry, but you are. That's why we hired you.

FRANK: They only hired me because I always get good reviews.

JAMES: That's a pretty good reason.

JULIA: And you're from Chicago, darling. Let's not forget that.

FRANK: I was born in New Jersey.

JULIA: We don't talk about that. You came to us from Chicago.

FRANK: I don't know what I'm doing!

JULIA: You don't?

FRANK: You wait and see: I'll win a Tony for this.

JULIA: Well, I certainly hope so.

JAMES: May I see your lighter?

FRANK: Why am I smoking? I don't smoke . . . I ate red meat tonight. *(He tosses James his lighter)*

JAMES: This is my lighter. Carol Burnett gave it to me.

FRANK: Prove it.

JAMES: Right there, the engraving. "All my love, Carol."

FRANK: Sorry. Carol Burnett gave it to me.

JAMES: Prove it.

FRANK: Right there, the engraving. "All my love, Carol." *(He pockets the lighter)*

JULIA: Maybe it is his lighter, James.

JAMES: A while ago I caught him stealing this box.

JULIA: Please, don't handle that. It's extremely delicate.

FRANK: It really means that much to you, man? Here, you can have mine.

JAMES: I don't want yours.

FRANK: See? You admitted it. *(He tosses the lighter to James)*

JAMES: Can we go down now, Julia?

FRANK: I am in despair, people.

JULIA: What kind of despair, Frank?

JAMES: *(A whimper)* Oh, my God!

FRANK: Deep despair. Life despair. Everything despair.

40

JULIA: This should be the biggest night of your life. A debut on Broadway at your age. How old are you?

JAMES: Julia, please.

FRANK: The Emperor isn't wearing any clothes!

JAMES: *(Anticipating/mimicking Julia)* What emperor, darling?

JULIA: What emperor, darling?

FRANK: This emperor. I'm a fake. My work's a fake. I can't go on like this—the critics' darling—knowing that it's all a fake.

JULIA: Try to hold on just one more time.

FRANK: I've had fourteen hits in a row Off-Broadway and thirty-seven Obies. I want a flop. I need a flop. Somebody, tell me, please: when is it my turn? I'm no good. You've got to believe me. I'm no good.

JAMES: We believe you. Julia, now can we go down—?

FRANK: Hold me.

JULIA: We can't leave him like this.

FRANK: Do you know the only flops I've ever had? At drama school. Nobody liked my production of anything. My Art Deco *Three Sisters.* My spoken *Aida.* My gay *Godot.* But what got me expelled was my *Titus Andronicus.* I did the whole thing in mime. No dialogue. No poetry. No Shakespeare.

JULIA: What did it have?

FRANK: Blood bags. Every time somebody walked on stage: splat! They got hit with a big blood bag. God, it was gross.

JULIA: It sounds interesting.

FRANK: It was terrible. But at least everyone said it was terrible. I'm pulling the same stunts in New York and everybody says it's brilliant.

JULIA: It is brilliant.

FRANK: I hate it! God I miss Yale.

JAMES: I'm sure Yale misses you.

FRANK: *(Emptying his pockets)* I don't want these things. Honest I don't. Please, don't leave them around.

JULIA: Frank, that's my good pepper shaker!

JAMES: May I see that?

(Julia and James are amazed at the size and diversity of Frank's haul)

FRANK: You know what my analyst says? "Put it back, Frank." Seventy-five bucks an hour and that's all she says. "Put it back, Frank."

JULIA: *(Reading an engraving)* "To Dr. Mildred Sturgeon, Ph.D." Who's Mildred?

FRANK: My fucking analyst! I wanna know why I pick it up in the first place.

JAMES: *(Reading from a cigarette case)* "Mary. You are the 'Sound of Music.' All our love. Dick and Oscar." He's a syndicate.

(Virginia comes into the bedroom)

VIRGINIA: That fucking Channel 7. That fucking faggot dyke hermaphrodite transsexual whatever the hell you call it they have for a critic.

JAMES: We missed Katie Kelly's review! *(To Frank)* This is all your fault. *(He turns on the television)* I fly in six thousand miles for an opening night and I can't even get the goddamn reviews.

TV ANNOUNCER: In other news tonight, a Boeing 747 jetliner filled to capacity—.

(James hits TV "muting" switch)

JAMES: *(To Frank)* I hope you're pleased with yourself.

VIRGINIA: I just told a roomful of people to shut the fuck up so they could hear Katie Kelly say, "Virginia Noyes stinks."

JAMES: I'm sure she didn't say, "Virginia Noyes stinks."

VIRGINIA: "Virginia Noyes stinks." You could hear a pin drop, she was smiling when she said it: "Virginia Noyes stinks."

FRANK: *(Going to comfort her)* Ginny.

VIRGINIA: You cast me!

FRANK: The best move I ever made with this play.

JULIA: Frank's right. You were wonderful, darling. No matter what happens with the critics, you must never forget that. You were wonderful.

VIRGINIA: Do I know you?

JULIA: It's Julia, darling, your producer.

43

VIRGINIA: Oh, yeah, right, hi, thanks. You want a hit? *(Handing Julia a joint)*

JULIA: *(Not taking it)* Don't ask silly questions. Of course I want a hit. Everyone at this party does. What did she say about the play?

VIRGINIA: "Good, solid theater."

JULIA: That's exactly what what's-his-name said.

VIRGINIA: Who?

JULIA: The one who reviews for Channel something-or-other-I-don't-know. Until tonight I never heard of these people.

(Gus appears with a load of yellow slickers)

JAMES: Don't tell me. *Singin' in the Rain.*

GUS: Is Felda Toeshoe anybody?

JULIA: Who?

GUS: That's what I thought.

JAMES: Everybody in the theater is somebody. I think that's probably the most pretentious thing I've ever said.

(Peter comes into the bedroom as Gus goes out)

PETER: They don't have a clue who I am down there. Colleen Dewhurst thought I was help and asked me to bring them a gin spritzer.

(Peter "sees" Frank)
There he is! My genius director. I'm difficult to work with and you're close to impossible. It's a marriage made in heaven and I'm sending you my next play.

FRANK: Next time I'll cut all the stage directions.

PETER: Next time I'll let you do all the rewrites. Why is that television not on? It's almost time. Has Buzz called? *(He is already dialing the number)* He should have some word on the *Times* by now. I guess you heard we've already gotten two raves?

JULIA: We did? That's wonderful. Who from?

PETER: Stewart Klein and Katie Kelly.

JULIA: They weren't raves, dear. They said we were "good, solid theatre."

PETER: That's pretty damn good, Julia. What do you want, blood?

JULIA: Buzz promised me the moon!

PETER: *(Into phone)* What are you telling this woman, Buzz?

VIRGINIA: Buzz Hepburn. The asshole press agent.

JULIA: He's at the top of his heap, Virginia.

VIRGINIA: Some heap.

PETER: *(Into phone)* Forget all that, Buzz. Any word on the *Times?* You're kidding! *(To the others)* He heard it's an out-and-out rave! He went crazy for us! *(Into phone)* You're sure? *(To others)* He bribed a copyboy. *(Into phone)* That's great, Buzz. *(To James)* Channel 2 is coming up. *(James will get the television set ready)* He says it's going to be unanimous.

JULIA: You see, Virginia?

VIRGINIA: I hope he's right.

45

PETER: Thanks, Buzz, I really appreciate that. *(He hangs up)* He says this play is proof you can still write a serious play for Broadway and have a house in the Hamptons as well. Actually, I've got my eye on something in Nantucket. I've always felt very close to Melville. *(He shivers)*

JULIA: What's the matter?

PETER: If we have a smash hit on our hands, I hope I can handle it. *(Frank makes a retching noise)* Better than you, anyway. You know what I'm going to do with my first royalty check? Buy this one four hundred of his own Mark Cross pens.

(James has turned up the television sound)

JAMES: Channel 2. Here we go. *(James waves the remote control at Frank)* I'm hanging on to this.

TV: Hi, theater lovers. This is Kevin Kunst filling in for our regular critic, who's out with a bug. That was no bug, he's gonna tell me. That was my wife. *(There is much hilarity in the television studio. Almost none in Julia's bedroom)*

JULIA: What are we watching?

PETER: Channel 2, Good Ol' Boy News.

TV: It was quite a kick for me to cover a big-time Broadway opening. I was sitting next to award-winning director Bob Fosse. I asked him what he thought. "Forget what I thought," Mr. Fosse laughed. "Let me tell you what—"

(James turns off the volume)

JAMES: I'm sorry. I never did know how these things work.

PETER: Give me that. *(He turns the sound back on. Again there is much hilarity in the television studio)*

46

TV: . . . "Gobble, gobble!" Anyway, for what it's worth, I thought Peter Austin's new play was the kind of good old-fashioned play nobody writes anymore except Peter Austin. But what do I know?

PETER: Not very much. That is the face of an imbecile.

TV: This is Kevin Kunst. Channel 2, Good Ol' Boy News.

TV (SECOND VOICE): In other news tonight, and this is just in, a packed Roosevelt Island Cable Car—

(Peter turns the sound down)

PETER: I'd call that mixed.

JULIA: I'd call it lousy. What did I ever do to Kevin Kunst? Who is he? What is he? How dare he?

VIRGINIA: You want a downer?

PETER: God, I want a cigarette.

VIRGINIA: Do the wires.

FRANK: I still don't believe it and I've seen it a hundred times.

JAMES: What does he have in there?

VIRGINIA: Little wire staples. When he presses them, they send a message to the nerve ends and he doesn't want to smoke.

JULIA: Acupuncture sounds horrible.

VIRGINIA: It's fucking fabulous. I used it to get off drugs.

(The phone rings. Peter will answer it. Gus enters with more coats)

47

JULIA: Now who?

GUS: *The Iceman Cometh and Mavens.*

JULIA: *Mavens?*

JAMES: A new musical that's opening next month. They start previews this weekend.

JULIA: They've got some nerve. Didn't *Iceman* close?

VIRGINIA: Yes, but nobody's told them yet.

PETER: Stop the presses! He's got new quotes. "Hats off and hallelujah. Peter Austin has written the best American play since *The Man Who Had Three Arms.* Virginia Noyes lights up Broadway."

VIRGINIA: You bet your fucking A I do!

PETER: "Frank Finger's direction is superb, taut and just plain perfect."

FRANK: That's it?

PETER: "Along with David Mamet, Sam Shepard, Michael Weller, Albert Innaurato, David Rabe, John Guare, Wendy Wasserstein, Tina Howe, Christopher Durang, Ted Talley, David Henry Hwang, Beth Henley, Lanford Wilson, Marsha Norman, A. R. Gurney, Jr., Wallace Shawn, Ntozake Shange and Hugh Golden . . ."

THE OTHERS: Who?

PETER: "Peter Austin is in that small handful of our more promising young American dramatists."

JULIA: Amen.

PETER: The *Newark* News. Thanks, Buzz. How much longer before we get Rich? Very funny. Another half hour? *(He hangs up)* We're a smash in Newark.

JULIA: That was a wonderful review.

PETER: Not if you're David Mamet, John Guare, Sam . . . *(He sees a new picture on the television set)* Channel 7! *(He turns up the sound)*

TV: For what it's worth, I'd call this the best American play of the season, hands down.

(They all cheer and hug)

VIRGINIA: Right on!

JULIA: I hope Elliott is watching. He had doubts.

JAMES: No!

JULIA: Real doubts.

TV: In the excellent cast, Jane Bergere is brilliant as the shepherdess.

PETER: What shepherdess?

VIRGINIA: Who the fuck is Jane Bergere?

TV: In short, at least in this workshop production, Robert Patrick's new play scores a clear home run. Back to you, Carmen.

TV (SECOND VOICE): Two-time Academy Award winner singer/actress Barbra Streisand was found—

(Peter turns off the sound)

JAMES: Something about Barbra!

PETER: Thank God we know the *Times* is a rave.

JAMES: Something happened to Barbra Streisand!

PETER: The television didn't like *Flashes,* either.

JAMES: Doesn't anybody care?

PETER: At this point, five years ago, we were all suicidal.

JAMES: I'm still suicidal. Give me that. *(He takes the remote control)*

PETER: I don't know about anyone else, but I am going to have some of that gorgeous food I saw down there. Julia?

JULIA: I don't think so.

PETER: James?

JAMES: I want to find out what happened to Barbra.

PETER: Ginny? Frank?

VIRGINIA: Once was enough. If you see Paul Verrano, tell him I'm up here.

FRANK: Is that who you're with? He's gay.

VIRGINIA: I know. Who are you with?

FRANK: No one.

VIRGINIA: So look who's talking.

JAMES: I give up.

PETER: It can't be that important.

JAMES: Anything that happens to Barbra is important.

PETER: I want you to do me a favor down there. Ask Walter Kerr what he thought.

JAMES: Are you crazy?

PETER: I have a feeling he liked it.

JAMES: He never has before.

PETER: I had a mass said for them.

JAMES: Peter.

PETER: They know I had a mass said for them. I sent a mass card. *(Peter leaves)*

JAMES: You know, I wouldn't put it past him.

(There is the sound of a window breaking from behind the closed drapes)

JAMES: What was that?

JULIA: It sounded like the window.

(Julia, James, Frank and Virginia go to the window and pull back the drapes. There is a broken pane, shattered glass on the carpet and a snowball)

JULIA: Do you see anyone?

JAMES: Across the street. *(Yelling at them)* What's the matter with you? Are you crazy? Look out! *(Another snowball is thrown)* This would never happen in California.

FRANK: Who are they? Street toughs?

JULIA: It's the cast of *Annie*.

JAMES: Are you sure?

JULIA: I'm a principal investor.

(There is a commotion from downstairs)

JULIA: Now what?

JAMES: It sounds like a brawl.

JULIA: All I did was produce a play on Broadway and give an opening-night party!

JAMES: Welcome to the theater.

JULIA: What's happening down there?

(Julia and James leave the bedroom)

FRANK: You want to split?

VIRGINIA: If I had any sense I would.

(Ira Drew rushes in. He is holding his mouth with a handkerchief)

IRA: Bathroom?

(Frank indicates the bathroom. Ira enters it. He is promptly set upon by Torch)

FRANK: Is that who I think it is?

VIRGINIA: If it is, score one for our side.

(Julia rushes back in)

52

JULIA: Where is he? Where's Mr. Drew?

(There is the sound of a gunshot from the bathroom. Julia screams. Frank and Virginia jump)

FRANK: What the fuck was that?

JULIA: Noooooooooooooooo!

(The bathroom door opens. Ira comes out. His pants legs are in shreds. He is still dabbing at his mouth with his handkerchief. He carries a pistol)

IRA: I guess that's your dog.

JULIA: Murderer. Mur-der-er! *(She hurls herself at Ira and beats him with her fists)*

IRA: I didn't shoot him. He's perfectly all right.

JULIA: He'd better be. Torch! Darling Torch! *(She goes into bathroom)*

IRA: Darling? It's the last remaining Hound of the Baskervilles. Look at me.

FRANK: Is that thing real?

IRA: Don't worry. It's loaded with blanks. I had to start carrying it in self-defense. I'm Ira Drew. Good evening, Miss Noyes. I enjoyed your performance. I liked your work too, Mr. Finger, but then I always do. *Titus Andronicus.* Splat.

FRANK: Looks like somebody decked you.

IRA: Your playwright.

FRANK: Peter took a swing at you?

IRA: Mr. Austin took several swings at me. The next thing I knew I was on the floor and Linda Hunt was kicking me.

FRANK: This I gotta see.

IRA: You're too late. *(But Frank is gone)* That's right, Mr. Finger adores violence.

VIRGINIA: I guess that's it for your review.

IRA: Nothing is going to affect my review. Critics can't afford to hold petty grudges. Your playwright's only human, the little shit.

VIRGINIA: You just said—

IRA: Just because I think someone's a little shit doesn't mean I'm going to give him a bad review. My sole responsibility as a critic is to objectively evaluate what the little shit's written.

VIRGINIA: In print you describe yourself as a Humanist.

IRA: I am a Humanist. I just happen not to like most people! *(He laughs. Julia comes out of the bathroom)* How is he?

JULIA: He'll be right up to apologize.

IRA: I meant Grendel in the cave.

JULIA: He's fine. I don't understand. He's never turned on anyone before. I'm so disappointed in him tonight. Thank God you missed. I don't know what I would have done.

VIRGINIA: So what did you think of the play tonight?

JULIA: Mr. Drew doesn't have to answer that question.

VIRGINIA: Why not?

JULIA: He's a critic. We have to wait to read what he writes. It's very rude to ask.

IRA: If you'd rather wait for my piece . . . !

VIRGINIA: He was going to tell us.

IRA: Besides, waiting for the *Times*, that's what tonight's all about. Who cares what a nonentity like me thinks?

JULIA: You're not a nonentity and you're very well thought of.

IRA: Not well enough apparently for a performance scheduled to begin this evening at six forty-five sharp to begin at six forty-five sharp because the critic from the *Times* wasn't in his seat.

JULIA: Well, with this blizzard . . .

IRA: It snows for all of us, Mrs. Budder. Then, just as I'm lighting another cigarette and wondering whether John Simon minds being so unpopular, a stretch cab pulls up, the *Times* pops out and there's a stampede towards the theater. By the time I get to my seat, the play's already begun. I don't want Mr. Rich's job. [I'll take his seat location.] I just want to finish my cigarette. I am sounding petty.

JULIA: Nonsense. It's good for a producer to hear these things—!

IRA: All right! I am sick and tired of half the audience, every time there is a laugh line, turning around in their seats to see if he is laughing. I have been reviewing plays for eighteen years and no one has ever, not once, turned around in their seat to see if I were laughing.

JULIA: That's the saddest thing I ever heard.

IRA: I saw you peeping at him through the side exit curtains tonight, Mrs. Budder.

JULIA: I wasn't peeping at him, Mr. Drew. I swear to God, I wasn't peeping.

IRA: Don't deny it, Mrs. Budder.

JULIA: All right, yes, I was!

IRA: What am I? The Invisible Man?

VIRGINIA: You're one of the most vicious critics in New York.

IRA: Throw that in my face. I love the theater; it's what people are doing to it I can't stand.

JULIA: It's not on purpose.

VIRGINIA: "She reminds me of nothing so much as a female impersonator in search of a female to impersonate."

JULIA: What a dreadful thing to say about anyone.

IRA: I said that about Norma Bird in *The Sea Gull* at the Provincetown Playhouse in 1968. It's curious you remember that.

VIRGINIA: I was Norma Bird in *The Sea Gull* at the Provincetown Playhouse in 1968.

JULIA: You changed your name?

VIRGINIA: After his review I changed my face.

IRA: I'm sorry. I had no idea I'd—

VIRGINIA: Face it, you don't like anything!

56

IRA: That's not true and a lot of good it does me when I do. Who of you remembers my rave review for *Windswept?*

JULIA: *Windswept?*

IRA: I said it was the best American play since *Leaf People.*

JULIA: *Leaf People?*

(Peter enters with Frank)

PETER: I'm sorry, Mr. Drew. Deeply and truly and terribly sorry.

IRA: Just as you're entitled to write your plays, I'm entitled to my opinion of them.

PETER: *(As they shake hands)* Fair enough. *(Peter drops to his knees, still holding Ira's hand)* Hear a playwright's prayer, O Lord. Listen to the humble plea of thy humble servant Peter, descendant of Aeschylus, Shakespeare, Molière, Ibsen, Chekhov, O'Neill and Pinter.

FRANK: What the hell is he doing?

PETER: Bless me and my meager skills with which I've only tried to amuse, intrigue, provoke, stimulate and move You and an audience while creating believable characters in true-to-life situations which somehow illuminate the human experience.

JULIA: *(Touched)* Oh, Peter!

PETER: Bless thy humble producer-servant Julia.

JULIA: *(Sinking to her knees)* How lovely!

PETER: Bless all producers who put our plays on and keep them running even when it means enormous financial sacrifice.

JULIA: I don't care about that, Peter, you know I don't.

PETER: Bless her and forgive her her choice of press agent.

VIRGINIA: You hear that, Julia?

PETER: Bless thy humble actress-servant Virginia, who gave the performance of a lifetime tonight.

JULIA: Get down, Virginia!

PETER: Bless her unique timing, her wonderful voice, her way with a prop.

VIRGINIA: It slipped, Peter.

PETER: Bless her for being almost letter perfect in her part.

VIRGINIA: Will you lay off?

PETER: Bless thy humble director-servant Frank.

FRANK: (Self-conscious) Oh, Christ.

PETER: Bless him for returning my raincoat, which so mysteriously vanished the second day of rehearsal. Bless him for his unbroken string of successes. Bless all directors with an unbroken string of successes.

(James enters)

JAMES: The food is wonderful . . .

PETER: Bless my best friend, James, thy humble television series star-servant, who had to turn my play down and so we came up with Jack, for whom everyone says there is a definite Tony nomination, if not award, in this. Bless Jack and his Tony nomination, if not award. Also bless James's series, which is rumored to be going off the air.

58

JAMES: Where did you hear that?

VIRGINIA: Liz Smith, "Live at Five."

JULIA: Quiet!

(James has gotten to his knees during this. Only Ira is still standing. He is clearly opposed to joining the others on the floor, but Peter is really putting him on the spot)

PETER: Bless thy humble critic-servant Ira. Bless him for writing the one and only pan of my first play, *Flashes*, which all the other critics loved and made me rich and famous, which made him look like something of a fool and which is why I hit him. *(Ira is about to protest)* Bless this good man, Lord. Bless my . . . dare I say it? . . . my newest friend. Bless all critics who mean well and are only trying to uphold the standards of the theater without knowing how truly hard it is to write a play. Shower them with the same mercy they deny others. And bless the theater in which we all serve. Bless this ancient art which is so superior to the movies.

JULIA: The theater, yes!

(Gus has come upstairs and entered the bedroom)

GUS: Mrs. Budder.

JULIA: Get down, Gus!

GUS: *(Kneeling)* I'm also supposed to be getting Lauren Bacall her coat.

PETER: Bless thy humble servant-servant . . . what's your name, love?

GUS: Gus.

PETER: Gus, who is bringing Betty Bacall's coat down to her. Bless Betty. Bless all those people down there whose happiness and approval mean so much to me. Bless Hal and Judy and Steve, Josh and Nedda, Betty and Adolph, even dear Rex and poor Sylvia.

IRA: Who is Sylvia? Damn it, I fell for it.

PETER: And finally, Lord, bless the taxi driver who dropped me off here and who this very minute is waiting at the *Times* with the meter running, ready to race back here with their review . . . *(An audible shiver of excitement runs through the kneeling group)* Bless this driver. Bless their review.

JULIA: Amen!

PETER: *(Just as the others are about to get up)* Lord! In our hour of greatest need, give us . . . you who have given me the greatest gift of all, the gift to realize that no matter what happens tonight, it's only a play . . . give us just one more thing. It's not much. When you consider the problems you've unleashed on this world: wars and famines and jet-plane crashes, surely you can give us a hit tonight. If you can't give us unanimous raves, we'll settle for the *Times*. The rest are negotiable. That is my prayer to you, Lord. That is every playwright's prayer.

JULIA: Amen.

THE OTHERS: *(Muttered)* Amen.

PETER: Do you hear me, Lord, may I hope for some sign?

(The telephone begins to ring)

GUS: That was quick. *(Picks up phone)* Hello? *(To James)* It's for you.

JAMES: Who on earth could that be? Hello?

60

IRA: You know, Mr. Austin, there was a genuine sincerity when you spoke.

PETER: That surprises you?

IRA: From the author of this evening's play, quite frankly, yes.

JULIA: I'm so glad to see you two getting along.

IRA: It's the funniest thing. I like you personally.

JULIA: We all do.

IRA: It's just your work I can't stand. Now, you take someone like David Mamet and I have the totally opposite reaction.

(Peter is upon him! In a flash he has his hands around Ira's throat and is trying to do him great harm. Virginia and Frank are taking coke)

VIRGINIA: Hit it, hit it!

JULIA: Peter! Gentlemen! Stop that, please!

IRA: Help! Help!

(James is having his own problems on the telephone)

JAMES: Canceled? My series has been canceled?

JULIA: Will somebody do something? *(Julia is turning in circles)*

FRANK: *(Holding the spoon for Virginia)* Hit it, Ginny, hit it!

(Emma Stewart is seen coming up the stairs. She is wearing a leather jacket, jeans and a cloth cap. She comes into the bedroom. This is what she sees: Peter straddling and strangling Ira, Julia running in hysterical circles, Virginia and Frank doing

61

coke, James in a state approaching catatonia. Emma puts two fingers in her mouth and whistles. It is a loud whistle. Everyone stops what they are doing and looks at her)

EMMA: Hey you!

PETER: What?

EMMA: You know that paper you're waiting on?

ALL (EXCEPT JAMES): Yes!

EMMA: The one with the review?

ALL: Yes!!

EMMA: The New York *Times?*

ALL: Yes!!!

EMMA: They got it down there.

(Total chaos. Emma is knocked over in their surge to get downstairs and get that paper)

EMMA: What's wrong with these people? It's only a play!

(The curtain is falling. James looks like something out of the Last Judgment. All the phones on Julia's desk have started ringing. Torch is barking and tearing at the bathroom door)

END OF ACT I

ACT TWO

o o o o o o o o o

ACT II

AT RISE: *The same as Act I, a few moments later. James is seated by the telephone, clutching his head in despair. Gus is looking through piles of coats. Emma is brushing herself off. Torch is still savaging the bathroom door. All the phones are ringing.*

GUS: *(To the phones)* Hold your horses!

EMMA: *(To James)* All I said was "Here's your paper." What's the matter with those people?

JAMES: Do you mind? I have my own problems.

GUS: *(Snatching up the house phone)* Yes? . . . Tell Miss Bacall I'm looking for her coat! *(He hangs up and continues to search)*

EMMA: *(To James)* I know you.

JAMES: Please.

EMMA: Don't worry. I'm cool. I've had celebrities up the kazoo in my back seat. I respect their privacy and I expect them to respect mine. "Top of the morning to you, Mrs. Onassis," and that's it until she gets out. Then it's "Have a good one, Mrs. O." I like 'em to know that I know but that's it. You dig? Now of course you take someone like Howard Cosell, who's a real chatterbox, and it's a whole other thing.

JAMES: I'll sell the house and do a new Neil Simon play. If Doc doesn't have a new play, I'll go out with *Charley's Aunt* again.

GUS: *(Snatching up the phone again)* You're out of food down there? Call Chicken Delight! *(He hangs up and continues to search)*

65

EMMA: See, celebrities are just like anybody else. They just happen to be famous. I could be Lucille Ball, only I'm not. Big deal.

GUS: *(Snatching up an outside line this time)* Yeah? . . . Anybody here put in a call to Carol Burnett? *(James breaks down and cries)*

EMMA: I'll talk to her.

GUS: Wrong number. *(He hangs up)*

EMMA: Is it always like this around here?

GUS: I wouldn't know. I'm temporary.

EMMA: I'm Emma.

GUS: I'm Gus.

EMMA: Emma, Emma Bovary. It's a long story. We all have a cross to bear. Listen, it could have been Hitler, you know? Emma Hitler. Count your blessings, that's what I always say. What are we looking for?

GUS: Lauren Bacall's mink. *(Emma will help him search for the coat)*

JAMES: Does anybody know if *The Mousetrap* has ever been done in America? *(Peter, Julia, Virginia, Frank, and Ira are tearing up the stairs. They have the New York* Times, *only it is in several sections. As they come pouring into the room, a desperate battle ensues. These people will stoop to anything to get their hands on that review. Think of children in a sandbox)*

PETER: Give me that.

IRA: Let go.

VIRGINIA: That's mine.

JULIA: It's my house.

IRA: Fight fair.

PETER: Go write your own review.

JAMES: I just want the television page.

PETER: It's my paper. I sent for it.

FRANK: Why didn't you get two?

PETER: I didn't know so many crazy people would be fighting over it.

FRANK: You're ripping it.

IRA: Give me that. *(They rip the section in half)*

FRANK: Now look what you've done. *(Emma steps forward)*

EMMA: We're missing a mink up here.

PETER: You!

EMMA: Don't worry. I've stopped the meter.

PETER: Just tell me what he said.

EMMA: What who said?

PETER: The *Times,* the *Times,* the *Times!!*

EMMA: I don't read the *Times,* the *Times,* the *Times!!* What do I look like? I'm a *News* reader. *(She has made the mistake of taking the* News *out of her back pocket)*

PETER: *(Snatching it)* Give me that!

EMMA: *(Snatching it right back)* No!

PETER: Please!

EMMA: Well, don't grab. *(She gives it to him)* Here. Half an hour ago you were a nice young man.

PETER: Tell me about it. *(Throwing the paper down)* It's an early edition. There's no review.

JAMES: Doesn't anybody have the television page?

VIRGINIA: It's not here.

JULIA: It has to be here.

JAMES: Here it is! *(Everyone freezes)* "ABC Announces Four Cancellations; 'Out on a Limb' Among Them."

(The frenzied search resumes as James crosses to sit and read the television page)

EMMA: Aw! I liked that show.

FRANK: Wait. Listen to this. "For reasons of space, Frank Rich's review of last night's opening at the Barrymore appears today on page seventy-six under 'Dogs, Cats, and other Pets.'"

PETER: They buried us.

FRANK: Who has seventy-six? *(There is much rustling of newspaper)*

IRA: I've got one through nine and then they're all in the thirties.

VIRGINIA: *(Struck by a news item)* Jesus! *(Again they all freeze)*

ALL: What?

VIRGINIA: *The Fantasticks* is closing.

PETER: Fuck *The Fantasticks.*

JULIA: What page are we looking for?

ALL: *(Apoplectic)* Seventy-six!

JULIA: *(With great dignity. She is not to be shouted at like this. Ever.)* I produced this play and I can close it. *(She calmly checks her page numbers)* Now, let me see. Page seventy-four, "Consumer Notes." Page seventy-five, "Wine Talk."

PETER: It's Chinese torture.

JULIA: Will you people stop crowding me? Thank you. Here we are. Page seventy-six! *(They descend on her, snatching the precious page)* Be careful! *(Peter wins. The paper is his)*

PETER: Now, everybody sit down.

EMMA: Me, too?

PETER: Sit down and shut up. You shouldn't even be here.

EMMA: I know. You want me to go?

PETER: No!

JAMES: *(Throwing his section of the* Times *aside)* We never had a chance.

PETER: That goes for you, too.

JAMES: Not with our writers.

PETER: James.

JAMES: Not in our time slot.

PETER: Jimmy!

JAMES: Not with her for a costar. *(He has gone to the telephone)*

PETER: What are you doing?

JAMES: *(Already dialing)* There are other things in the world besides your play.

PETER: Not for the next five minutes there are not.

JAMES: *(Into phone)* Hello, ABC? I represent eight hundred Italian Catholics in the Bronx and I want to protest the cancellation of—

(Peter breaks the connection)

PETER: This is my moment and you're not going to spoil it.

JAMES: You could stuff a moose with the egos in this room.

GUS: *(Taking this as a cue to sit)* Miss Bacall says she's not leaving till she gets her coat back. Neither is Leonard Bernstein.

JULIA: *(On the house phone)* I can't talk to you when you get like this, Betty. *(She hangs up)*

PETER: May I have silence? *(The phones have begun to ring again. Peter will take them all off the hook)* Until we finish, there will be no interruptions.

VIRGINIA: Don't be so dramatic, Peter.

PETER: Drama is my business, lady.

JAMES: You could have fooled me.

70

PETER: Who said that? Who said that?

JAMES: I did. God, I wish I did drugs.

PETER: *(All ready to read)* Ahem!

VIRGINIA: Will you just read it, Peter?

PETER: *(After taking a deep breath)* "*Golden Egg* opens at the Barrymore."

VIRGINIA: We know what the name of your play is.

PETER: And then there's a smaller headline: "Actor scores brilliant triumph." That'll be Jack.

VIRGINIA: I knew it, I knew it. That's the part.

PETER: "With *The Golden Egg,* which opened last night at the blah blah blah, Peter Austin makes his eagerly awaited Broadway debut."

JULIA: It's a rave! I knew it!

PETER: *(He stops)* I can't.

JULIA: Peter!

PETER: I'm sorry, everyone. I'm too nervous. You, the cab driver. What's your name?

EMMA: Emma.

PETER: You read it.

EMMA: Emma Bovary.

PETER: Skip it.

71

EMMA: *(Taking the paper from him)* You're right. I'm the only objective person here.

GUS: I'm objective.

EMMA: I'm more. Now, everybody sit. *(Peter sits. Emma reads the review)*

PETER: Well?

EMMA: I'm reading, I'm reading!

PETER: Out loud! *(He grabs paper from her)*

EMMA: What am I? A mind reader?

PETER: Here. What's-your-name. You read it. *(Gus takes the paper and begins to read very haltingly)*

GUS: "With *The Golden Egg*, which opened last night at the—

PETER: Oh, give me that! *(He snatches it from him)* Where was I . . . ? *(He finds his place)* ". . . Peter Austin makes his eagerly awaited Broadway debut. Would that he hadn't." *(He looks up)* It's going to be mixed. *(He resumes)* "This is the kind of play that gives playwriting a bad name and deals the theatre, already a somewhat endangered species, something very close to a death blow." *(He looks up)* I don't think he liked it.

VIRGINIA: Peter.

PETER: I'm okay, Ginny, I'm okay. *(Resumes)* "It tarnishes the reputation of everyone connected with it, not permanently perhaps, but certainly within their lifetime."

JULIA: That sentence doesn't even make sense. What's more permanent than your lifetime?

PETER: "Even the usherettes and the concessionaires at the Barrymore should be walking with lowered heads today and for at least another season to come."

EMMA: When they go for the ushers! That's gotta be a first.

PETER: "Shame, ladies and gentlemen of the cloakroom, shame." *(He looks up)* I'm going to be sick.

EMMA: *(Her hand out for the paper)* You don't want me to . . . ?

PETER: I began it and I'll finish it. *(Perhaps a wild howl escapes from him at this point, perhaps not)* "Any play that calls itself *The Golden Egg* is just asking for it." The title is a metaphor, an ironic metaphor.

EMMA: I don't know what an ironic metaphor is. I just know a lousy title when I hear one.

PETER: Who is this person anyway?

EMMA: The salt of the earth. Now, are you going to finish that? We're on pins and needles.

PETER: *(Resuming)* "With such a title, I must confess that I arrived at the playhouse with my critical hackles already up."

JULIA: He's admitting he was prejudiced.

PETER: "After ten minutes of Mr. Austin's play, they were so up the woman behind me complained she couldn't see. Lucky lady." *(He looks up)* You think this is easy? *(He resumes)* "If *The Golden Egg* is not the worst American play since *Pinched Nerve*, it is not for Mr. Austin's lack of trying. Better luck next time." Would you think any less of me if I burst into tears? *(He lets the review fall as Julia comforts him. Ira snatches it up)*

JULIA: My darling Peter.

73

IRA: "It is dismaying to remember that Mr. Austin—"

JULIA: Please, Mr. Drew!

PETER: It's all right, I can take it.

JULIA: You're only tormenting yourself.

PETER: Maybe I want to.

IRA: ". . . was the author of *Flashes*, which I praised to the skies along with my colleagues with the single exception of Ira Drew, who I generally find the least perceptive and the most prejudiced of the New York critics." *(He looks up)* That's a little dig. *(He resumes)* "Were we all wrong? Was Mr. Drew a prophet crying in the wilderness? I think so now and my apologies to Mr. Drew . . ." *(He looks up)* He's trying to make it up to me now. Too late, Frankie. *(He resumes)* ". . . whom I still regard as the least perceptive, most prejudiced, physically unappetizing and generally creepy drama critic in New York." *(He looks up)* I knew Frank didn't like me, but the *extent!*

JAMES: *(Reaching for the paper)* Are you going to finish the review or not?

IRA: *(Resuming in fury)* "The plot of Mr. Austin's debacle . . ."

JAMES: We know all that.

VIRGINIA: Get to the acting.

IRA: "I can be more cheerful about the acting."

VIRGINIA: I should hope so.

74

IRA: "But not much. Only Jack Nimble, as the unlucky Tamburini, a role that was clearly tailored for James Wacker—"

JAMES: Wicker!

IRA: It says, "Wacker." *(He resumes)* "—emerges with distinction. If there is any justice in our theatre, and I am becoming less and less convinced that there is—How can there be, when plays like this get produced?"

PETER: Leave me alone, goddammit!

IRA: "Then, Mr. Nimble is a shoo-in for this season's Best Actor Tony Award."

JAMES: A what?

IRA: "As for Mr. Wicker—"

JAMES: What did I do?

IRA: They got it right this time. *(He resumes)* "—who is chiefly remembered hereabouts for his somewhat overpraised performance in Mr. Austin's *Flashes*—"

JAMES: For my what?

IRA: Somewhat overpraised performance. *(He resumes)* "Certainly I preferred his replacement, Charles Nelson Reilly, who brought a more masculine presence and yet strangely cutting sensitivity to the role."

JAMES: A more what?

JULIA: *(Always helpful)* A more masculine presence and—

JAMES: Shut up, Julia. I heard what he said.

75

IRA: ". . . he should count himself lucky to be out of this turkey due to his commitments to his enormously popular television series (I must admit I'm mad for it, but don't tell my colleagues) 'Out on a Lamb.'"

JAMES: "Limb," dammit, "Limb."

IRA: It says, "Lamb."

JAMES: Give me that! *(He furiously snatches the paper)*

VIRGINIA: That's funny, I thought I was the star of this thing.

JAMES: Don't worry, honey, he'll get to you. He went bananas tonight. *(He reads)* "Virginia Noyes, making one would have thought a welcome return to the New York stage after an ill-starred stint in Hollywood, wears out her welcome in her first speech."

VIRGINIA: I don't have a speech. I only have three lines.

JAMES: "She reminded this poor groundling of nothing so much as a female impersonator in search of a female impersonator to impersonate."

IRA: That's almost out-and-out plagiarism.

VIRGINIA: Jesus.

JAMES: "I hope, by the time she reads this, she is headed back to Burbank. Bon voyage and good riddance, Miss Noyes." *(He looks up)* Why, that's terrible, just terrible.

EMMA: I wouldn't be in the theater if you paid me.

JAMES: "The rest of the cast is outstanding."

JULIA: Now, that's more like it.

76

JAMES: "Considering what these valiant troupers have been asked to perform, I'm only surprised they haven't marched on the producer's house and stoned it."

JULIA: He put them up to it.

JAMES: "As for the producer, one Julia Budder, and I urge you to remember that name, Julia Budder, remember it well, Julia Budder—"

JULIA: Stop, this is inhuman!

JAMES: "The *Playbill* tells us that this is her first independent production after many years as an extremely successful investor."

JULIA: I don't see what that has to do with the price of fish.

JAMES: "With the money she has made from these other shows, Mrs. Budder should have done something worthwhile: such as open a mental hospital in which to have her head examined."

JULIA: I have opened hospitals. I've done a lot for charity.

JAMES: "When one thinks of the plays Mrs. Budder could have produced, a Lanford Wilson—"

JULIA: I'm going to.

JAMES: "Or a Hugh Golden . . ."

JULIA: Who is he? I'll do him.

JAMES: ". . . instead of Mr. Austin's dreck, the mind boggles." *(He looks up)* Does anyone want to take over? *(He resumes)* "Not only was her decision to mount this play imbecilic, it was also immoral. What possessed you, Mrs. Budder?"

77

JULIA: What possessed any of us?

JAMES: "What possessed any of you? Have I left anyone out?"

FRANK: Everyone's favorite director.

JAMES: "Oh, yes, the direction of Frank Finger."

FRANK: Here it comes. I've been expecting this a long time.

JAMES: "Long the most brilliant of our younger directors [his production of *Titus Andronicus* at Yale has attained legendary status in certain circles; wretched me, I didn't see it], Mr. Finger again gives us a stunning production. This is a man who can do no wrong and I am sure his wrong would be right."

FRANK: I never heard such bullshit.

VIRGINIA: You want to trade?

PETER: Congratulations, Frank.

JULIA: Bravo, darling, bravo.

JAMES: "I hope this review will not make you want to rush to the Barrymore Theatre."

IRA: Can't you just see the lines on Forty-seventh Street? *(He laughs; quickly catches himself)* I'm sorry.

JAMES: "Besides, I bet they're striking the scenery at the Barrymore this very moment."

JULIA: What does that mean? Striking?

EMMA: Taking it down.

JAMES: "Unless, of course, it hasn't already collapsed out of sheer embarrassment. Oh, well, onwards and upwards with the Arts." *(Short pause)* That's it. *(He lets the review drop to the floor and sits. No one moves. There is a long, gloomy pause now)*

PETER: I think it's important that we all love one another very, very much right now.

VIRGINIA: He didn't even say I was pretty. I always got pretty at least before.

JAMES: *(He will never really get over this)* Charles Nelson Reilly?

IRA: Seeing you people like this, the genuine hurt . . . I'm sorry more critics can't share this experience with me.

JULIA: Oh, fuck off! I'm sorry, Mr. Drew, but please!

GUS: Down home, we'd wipe a dude like that out. Your mama would pack a gun and go shoot the mother. How do you write something like that about somebody's child?

(There is a burst of applause from downstairs)

PETER: Listen! You hear that?

VIRGINIA: *Popular Mechanics* just came in. I heard they loved us.

PETER: Besides, I knew he wouldn't like it. His best friend's wife's sister's niece is a Catholic. And anyway, I can think of lots of hit shows that made it without a good review from the New York *Times*.

EMMA: You can?

PETER: Will you stay out of this? It never fails. At every opening, some total stranger manages to penetrate the inner sanctum. Opening night of *Flashes* it was a chiropodist from Long Island. Everybody thought he was with somebody else. It turned out he hadn't even seen the show. Remember, Jimmy?

JAMES: Charles Nelson Reilly?

FRANK: For what it's worth, guys, I'm very proud I did this play.

PETER: Coming from you, that's worth a lot.

FRANK: This play threatens a lot of people.

JULIA: It does? Now you tell me.

JAMES: Dom DeLuise I could accept, but Charles Nelson Reilly?

VIRGINIA: Who was it who said, "Where else but in the theater do you get to rehearse and rehearse for weeks and weeks just to make a horse's ass of yourself?"

IRA: Did someone say that? That's very funny. *(He stifles himself)* But did you hear the one about the terrible actor who was playing Hamlet? He'd barely begun "To be or not to be" when the audience began booing, throwing things, the works. Finally, the actor stepped forward and said, "I didn't write this shit." *(This time he can't control himself. The others look at him with much loathing)* "I didn't write this shit." *(He is writhing with laughter. Finally he is aware of the silence in the room and that he is at the center of it)* I'm sorry. But seriously, weren't you aware something like this might happen?

PETER: Nothing's happened! We got one lousy review. Big deal. We still have the other papers, the weeklies, the monthlies.

IRA: What about your preview audiences?

VIRGINIA: What about them? We had two and a half weeks of nurses, nuns and nitwits.

JULIA: Don't be bitter, Virginia. It doesn't become you.

EMMA: Are you a straight play or a comedy?

VIRGINIA: Don't look at me.

PETER: We're a comedy with serious overtones.

EMMA: There's your trouble. People don't like overtones.

PETER: Don't be so literal. You haven't even seen the play. All I'm saying is, We don't need the critics. We'll run because we've got word-of-mouth.

VIRGINIA: We've got hoof-and-mouth!

JULIA: Virginia! I hate pessimism. I hate it in real life and I hate it in the theater. That's why I'm a producer.

FRANK: Don't let them do this to you, Ginny.

VIRGINIA: They ain't doing nothing. They tried that number on me out in Hollywood. "You're only as good as your last picture," my agent told me. "Bullshit" I told him. "Nothing's as bad as my last three pictures but especially me. Just get me a job." "Ginny, I can't get you arrested. Cool out for a couple of years. Get married again." Me, Miss Two-Time Tony Award Winner! Miss Hot Shit Herself! They wouldn't touch me with a twenty-foot pole. And people wonder why I bottomed out? It took seeing my face on the front page of the *National Enquirer* after marriage number three ended for it to suddenly hit me: what am I doing out here? Standing in the check out line at the Arrow Market on Santa Monica wearing a dirty bathrobe and nothing else, that's where I remembered who I was! An actress, a fucking stage actress. Two days later, I packed everything I owned into my little red Mustang and burned rubber straight back to New York.

PETER: You did the right thing, Ginny.

VIRGINIA: I didn't let you down?

PETER: Are you crazy?

VIRGINIA: I gotta hear it. I gotta hear it a lot.

FRANK: Anytime.

VIRGINIA: Good thing I didn't know I'd already worn out my welcome on my first speech. *(She goes)*

JULIA: Virginia!

FRANK: I'll go. *(Frank goes)*

PETER: You still want to be in show business, Gus?

GUS: Oh, sure! Don't you?

EMMA: You're safer doing ninety miles an hour blindfolded on the Jersey Turnpike.

GUS: My teacher says we're acrobats of the gods, working without a net.

JULIA: Gus?

GUS: Yes, Mrs. Budder?

JULIA: The party.

GUS: I'm sorry, Mrs. Budder. I forget sometimes.

JULIA: We all do.

(Gus goes)

EMMA: Can I get anyone anything?

PETER: Not for me.

EMMA: You could all use some food. Besides, I'm feeling a bit peckish myself. I hate sitting still. Always have. Maybe that's why I'm a cab driver. No, that's not why. I like people too much. I like listening to their problems. I'm not much of a talker myself. I get a kick out of gab. I hope I don't run into anyone I know down there. Look at me. They're your peers but my fares. *(Emma goes)*

PETER: James?

JAMES: No.

PETER: For the last time: Will you please go down there and ask Walter Kerr what he thought or not?

JAMES: You are asking this somewhat overpraised ex-star of stage, screen and now television to go down there into that den of success and Charles Nelson Reillys and ask Walter Kerr what he thought of your play? Sure, I hope he peepee-cacas on it. *(James leaves to go downstairs)*

PETER: No wonder we haven't heard any more from Buzz! *(Peter has noticed that all the telephones are still off the hook. During the following, he will rush about the room putting the receivers back onto their cradles)* Just remember your promise to me, Julia. You'll put up a fight for this show.

JULIA: One good quote and I'll put up the biggest fight anybody ever saw.

PETER: You might be needing that blimp yet.

83

IRA: What blimp?

PETER: Our press agent hired the Goodyear blimp with quotes for the play.

IRA: What's he going to quote?

PETER: Our good reviews. And here they come! *(Almost all the phones have started ringing again. Peter snatches one up)* Budder residence, Mission Control. This is the playwright speaking. Who is this?

JULIA: I'm not at home to anyone but the Shubert Organization, TWA, a Mr. Yamamoto or Gloria Vanderbilt.

PETER: It's Lanford Wilson.

JULIA: Darling Lance! *(She will pick up an extension)*

PETER: "Darling Lance!"

IRA: Have you read Mr. Wilson's new play?

PETER: It's terrific. I hate it. *(To Julia)* Would you mind not tying up the phones, Julia? I'm sure Buzz is trying to get through.

JULIA: *(Into phone)* Lanford, you're hysterical. I can't talk to you when you get like this. *(To Peter)* He's worried I'm not going to produce his play now.

PETER: *(Snatching up an extension)* She's sick of the Talleys. Everybody is. *(He hangs up. Emma returns with a heaping plate of food for Peter and the others)*

EMMA: I just had a run-in with one of your guests. I said, "Listen, mister, I don't care if you're Ed Koch, I saw the shrimp first." *(She is offering Peter food)* Here.

PETER: I can't.

EMMA: Eat.

PETER: I—

EMMA: Eat, I said! *(To Ira)* You, too.

(James enters)

PETER: Did you see Walter Kerr?

JAMES: Yes.

PETER: What did he say?

JAMES: He's returning your mass card. You got another "good, solid theater." *The Wall Street Journal. (James goes to bathroom. Torch goes into action. James isn't having any, however)* Watch it, Buster.

PETER: I'm sick of "good, solid theater."

EMMA: What's wrong with it?

PETER: It's not enough anymore.

IRA: You actually sent Walter Kerr a mass card? Now I've heard everything.

PETER: Put a bag over your head and I'd fuck you for a good review.

IRA: I can see that. But a mass card?

JULIA: *(On the phone)* Now, do some rewrites, Lanford! . . . Any rewrites. I don't want another tonight on my hands. *(She hangs up)* He's so dear.

PETER: Dear? I'm dear. He's pushy.

EMMA: *(Answering another phone)* Hello? It's for you, Mrs. Budder.

JULIA: Who is it?

EMMA: It's a Hugh Golden.

JULIA: Who?

PETER: Hugh Golden. The *Times* wants you to produce his new play. What did they do? Run your number with that review? *(Snatching up extension)* You certainly didn't waste any time! She never heard of you either. *(He slams down his extension. Julia has already picked up hers)*

JULIA: Hello, Mr. Golden. This is a pleasure.

PETER: Where is Rita Chang when I need her? I want a cigarette. I need a cigarette. Somebody give me a cigarette.

IRA: *(Offering one)* Here you are.

PETER: Get away from me. That man is the devil.

IRA: I'm trying to understand what this experience must be like for you people.

PETER: I'll tell you in one word: not nice.

(We can almost see Ira count and start to correct Peter but think better of it. Almost)

JULIA: *(Into phone)* Of course I'd be interested in reading your new play, Mr. Golden. You'll bicycle it over tonight?

PETER: I'm sure Buzz is trying to reach us, Julia.

JULIA: *(Into phone)* All right then, Hugh.

PETER: Hugh? It's Hugh already?

JULIA: *(Into phone)* Onwards and upwards yourself! *(She hangs up)* He sounds very talented.

PETER: At what?

IRA: He's no Caroline Comstock, Mrs. Budder.

PETER: *(Playwriting makes strange bedfellows)* And Hugh! He's got her calling him Hugh!

JULIA: It's his name, darling.

EMMA: *(Taking another call)* Yes?

JULIA: I feel like a producer again. I've got the old adrenaline going.

EMMA: Neil Simon on three. Irene Fornés on six.

JULIA: *(She's on a winning streak)* I'll have to get back to you, Doc. You, too, Irene. *(She hangs up)* Playwrights! I am going to be the earth mother of the American theater and you will all be my children. Come to me. Give me your plays, I want to spread theater. Increase and multiply it. The sky's the limit. Watch out, Broadway, here comes Julia Budder!

(Emma has answered the extension nearest her)

EMMA: Joe Papp on five.

JULIA: *(Scooping the phone up in one extravagant gesture from her last speech)* Joseph, darling, how are you?

PETER: *(To Ira)* It's like my play never happened. *(Furious at himself)* Why do I keep talking to you?

87

EMMA: Harold Pinter on two?

PETER: *(Snatching up extension)* She said American theater! *(He hangs up)* Of all the chutzpah! *(Ira corrects his pronunciation)*

JULIA: *(Whose spirits have visibly wilted)* How large a donation were you thinking of, Mr. Papp? Of course I support an Offenbach in the Park Festival next summer. Don't bite my head off. I just didn't expect you to ask me to put my money where my mouth is tonight.

IRA: That's the kind of behavior which has gotten him where he is today, which is almost everywhere.

JULIA: *(Hanging up)* I can never say no to that man. He wants $30,000. Who is Offenbach? *(Julia will rip a check out of her ledger-sized checkbook)*

PETER: A dead French composer. I am a living American playwright. Why don't you give me $30,000.

JULIA: I'm trying to give you a hit.

PETER: Do you have to do that now?

JULIA: It's just money. Besides, he's on his way over for it.

PETER: How? On his dog sled! All the reviews aren't in yet, Julia.

JULIA: How many *p*'s in Papp?

PETER: Four. I'm still here, people. My play isn't over. I sense an avalanche. I feel an abandonment. I smell a stampede. *(Peter is pacing in furious circles. No one pays him any mind)*

GUS: *(Entering)* Can you come downstairs, Mrs. Budder? They're running out of everything!

IRA: Mrs. Budder, about *Bluestocking* . . . !

EMMA: Where do you keep your vacuum cleaner, lady?

JULIA: I don't know.

EMMA: I hate a room to get like this.

(James comes out of the bathroom)

JAMES: Bye-bye, Torch. Night-night. *(To the others)* It's amazing what a little Valium will do.

JULIA: James!

JAMES: Kidding! That dog just needs a strong authority figure.

EMMA: You all do. *(To Julia)* You think it's downstairs?

(Julia goes, followed by Ira and Emma. Peter will look up a telephone number in his pocket diary and dial it during the following)

PETER: Do they know what I turned down to write this play? The financial sacrifices I made? The screenplay for *Annie*. A mini-series on the life of Henry Winkler. He's had a very interesting life. A pilot for Mary Lou Retton. A chance to work with Franco Zeffirelli on the history of civilization. Don't tell me I didn't pay my dues to write this play. *(Into phone)* Hello! Did I wake you? Good. This is James Wicker.

JAMES: What are you doing?

PETER: I just read your review of the new Peter Austin play and I think you're full of shit. *(He hangs up)* I guess that's telling him.

JAMES: Who was that?

PETER: Frank Rich.

JAMES: Frank Rich?

PETER: You see what they're driving me to?

JAMES: Frank Rich??

PETER: You're not listening to me.

JAMES: Frank Rich! You listen to me. You call him right back and tell him that wasn't me.

PETER: I love you. You're my best friend. I don't want to do these things.

JAMES: I love you, too, and I don't want you doing them. Dial.

PETER: If it means that much to you!

JAMES: Of course it means that much to me.

(Peter is looking up the number again. Emma appears, pushing the vacuum cleaner)

EMMA: It was right across the hall.

PETER: Where's your famous sense of humor?

JAMES: I never had one. Ever. It was all a lie. Hurry up. Before he reviews me again. What are you doing with his number anyway?

PETER: I have all the critics' numbers.

JAMES: And they have yours! *(To Emma)* He called Frank Rich and said it was me!

EMMA: You see an outlet? *(She will begin to vacuum)*

PETER: *(Into phone)* Hello, Mr. Rich? That wasn't James Wicker who just woke you up and said you were full of shit.

JAMES: Thank you, God. It was Charles Nelson Reilly.

PETER: It was Lanford Wilson. *(He hangs up)* If I weren't a playwright, I'd be a very nice person.

JAMES: Grow up, Peter. Face facts. Your play is a flop. *(Realizes what he's said)* I mean—!

PETER: You've been waiting to use that word all evening.

JAMES: That's not true.

PETER: You're actually frothing at the mouth. Look at you. There's foam on your lips. Say it again. Say flop.

JAMES: This is ridiculous.

(At some point in what follows, Emma will turn off the vacuum and listen)

PETER: Say it.

JAMES: I don't have to say it.

PETER: Oh, a new tack! *(To Emma)* He's not saying flop. He's implying it.

JAMES: So are a lot of other people.

EMMA: You want me to leave?

PETER: No! God, if that isn't the ugliest word in the English language, Emma—flop!—I'd like to know what is.

JAMES: How about wishing someone and his fucking series a sudden and violent death?

91

PETER: I was hysterical when I wrote that note.

JAMES: Not half as hysterical as I was when Julia showed it to me.

PETER: "Love" was the operative word, don't you know that yet?

JAMES: I'm sorry but I fail to see any love in "you miserable, no-talent fruit."

PETER: First chance you get and you bring the conversation right back to yourself. You can't stand someone else being in the spotlight for a change.

JAMES: Considering the spotlight you're under tonight, not really.

PETER: Considering the state of your career, I don't blame you.

EMMA: Grown men!

JAMES: I never believed you when you said you liked my series.

PETER: I never even watched it.

JAMES: I wish I could say the same about your play.

PETER: You didn't like it?

JAMES: I turned it down, didn't I? When have I ever turned anything down? I do "Love Boat"s.

PETER: To think I made you a star.

JAMES: To think you what?

PETER: You heard me.

JAMES: Made me a star?

PETER: *Flashes* would have made anyone I let play it.

JAMES: I thought you wrote it for me.

PETER: I did. Only real stars wanted to do it.

JAMES: Name one.

PETER: I can name twenty.

JAMES: Why didn't you go with one of them?

PETER: It was your play.

JAMES: After I got through with it, it was. I should have gotten author's royalties.

PETER: And I was thinking of reviving it with you.

JAMES: Revive it with someone with a more masculine presence who cuts deeper.

PETER: You know something? He did.

JAMES: Funny it closed three weeks after I left and he went in.

PETER: If you'll remember, there was a big strike on at the time.

JAMES: United Parcel, for Christ's sake. Next thing you'll be telling us is this one flopped because it opened on Flag Day.

PETER: You realize this is a wrap for our friendship?

JAMES: Total.

PETER: Good. *(To Emma)* You're my witness.

EMMA: If I had a best friend, I'd cherish him.

PETER AND JAMES: So would I!

(Emma turns the vacuum back on as Julia and Ira return)

JAMES: I spilled the beans, Julia. He's all yours.

JULIA: What happened?

PETER: Something that should have happened five years ago.

JAMES: Ten!

JULIA: Emma! I have someone for that!

EMMA: *(Turning off the vacuum to hear)* What?

JULIA: Not now!

IRA: If I could just read you the one passage from the second act—

JULIA: You either! *(To Peter)* What about the rest of the reviews?

PETER: *(Shaking his head, looking at his watch)* Any minute now.

JULIA: Have the Shuberts called yet?

PETER: Those vultures.

JULIA: They want me to keep us open until someone called Charo is ready to come in.

JAMES: What's she coming in in?

JULIA: Some little Lorca play.

94

PETER: Close this play, Julia—!

JULIA: Who said anything—?

PETER: It's crossed your mind. Don't deny it.

JULIA: Well, of course it's crossed it. No one's that stupid.

(Frank comes into the room with Virginia and Gus)

VIRGINIA: Are we gonna run?

PETER: We're still waiting for the rest of the reviews.

VIRGINIA: *El Diario* loved us. They gave us two ears and the tail.

PETER: Are you okay?

VIRGINIA: Is there a choice?

(The phone rings. Peter darts for it)

PETER: Buzz? *(Handing the phone to Julia)* It's the Shuberts.

JULIA: Thank God. Maybe they can help us. *(She takes the phone)* Bernie, darling. We're in an absolute state of shock. Do you think we could find a way to lower our weekly operating costs? Maybe we could persuade the *Times* to lower their advertising rates? *(She covers phone)* He's laughing. *(Into phone)* Then what about all those stagehands who just stand around staring at a disk? It doesn't even move. And who are those men playing poker in the basement? But we're not a musical.

EMMA: You don't wanna go messing with the unions.

JULIA: What you're telling me, Bernie, is that no one at the Barrymore will take a salary cut. I thought they liked Peter's play. I don't see how asking the playwright to waive his royalties will solve our problems.

PETER: I already am. Thanks a lot, Bernie.

JULIA: Well, if your hands are tied, Bernie, what about mine? . . . Of course I don't want that on my conscience. *(She hangs up)*

PETER: What?

JULIA: If I close tonight, they'll give the Barrymore to *Leather Maidens of Amsterdam.*

PETER: What's that?

IRA: It's a Dutch porno film. I mean, I heard it's a Dutch porno film.

PETER: What happened to Charo?

JULIA: She's closing in Baltimore.

PETER: She gets to go out of town and I don't. It's not fair.

JULIA: The thought of that beautiful theater being turned into a house of pornographic film.

JAMES: Terrible. Just terrible.

EMMA: Amen. New York without a theater district might as well be Newark.

GUS: Heck, they can't tear any more theaters down. I haven't made my Broadway debut yet.

PETER: I'd hate to be in your shoes, Julia.

JULIA: They're your shoes too. They're everybody's.

(The phone rings. Emma answers it)

PETER: That'll be Buzz.

EMMA: Hello?

(They all seem to sense that this is "it")

JULIA: All we need is one strong quote and I'll run this play forever.

PETER: The rest of this season will do.

EMMA: It's your press agent with the rest of the reviews. *(Emma is holding the phone out)*

JULIA: *(Shaking her head)* I'm too nervous. James?

(James reluctantly starts for the phone)

PETER: The moment he's been waiting for.

JAMES: That's not true.

JULIA: He doesn't mean that.

(James takes the phone. Julia, Peter, Virginia and Frank hold hands)

JAMES: *(Into phone)* Listen, Buzz, I hope you've got some good news for us . . . Jimmy Wicker . . .

EMMA: I take shorthand. You want me to . . . ?

(Julia nods. Emma takes up pencil and paper)

JAMES: That review in the *Times* was a shaft out of left field. *You* were double-crossed? How do you think they felt? Okay, let's go. *(He will listen and repeat the following)* "In the final analysis, Mr. Austin's new play falls just short enough of the mark to fail utterly, however honorably." The *Daily News*.

PETER: I love you, too.

JAMES: "If and when the great American play is written, and I sometimes wish our playwrights would forget all about even trying to, Peter Austin could be its author, but not with this one."

FRANK: You hear that?

VIRGINIA: A review like that would keep me going for at least the rest of my life.

JAMES: "Virginia Noyes is a luminescent actress."

VIRGINIA: That sounds good.

FRANK: It is good.

JAMES: "Frank Finger's direction . . ."

FRANK: We know. Look, I don't enjoy this.

JAMES: ". . . escapes me, the play and the production."

FRANK: Escapes who?

JAMES: "Long the most overrated talent in the American theater . . ."

FRANK: Is he talking about me?

JAMES: "Mr. Finger is one emperor who isn't wearing any clothes."

FRANK: He took the words right out of my mouth.

98

JAMES: Clive Barnes. The New York *Post.*

JULIA: Congratulations, Frank.

FRANK: Thanks.

VIRGINIA: Are you okay?

FRANK: I'm fine. So. Here I am. Here we are. Fuck. Hell, he's right, the little Cockney Limey. Give them a Green Card and they think they own the world. I got what I wanted. I'm not angry. I'm happy. You want to see anger? That's anger. You want to see happy? That's happy. *(They're the same)* Who does he think he is, anyway? My father? Oh, wow! Get in touch with this. You're having a breakthrough. Father! Critics! Good boy! Bad boy! Spank! Ouch! Hug! Oo! Puppets! Basement! Daddy! Yes! *(He is having a breakthrough: psychic fireworks abound. Finally, he grows still)* I had a breakthrough. Thank God I've got Mildred tomorrow. Here. *(He unloads more purloined goods)* Thank you, Clive.

VIRGINIA: You okay now?

FRANK: Terrific.

(They hug. Frank laughs easily.)

JAMES: Yes, we're still here, Buzz. You've made one person happy.

PETER: What about the weeklies?

JAMES: *(Quoting Buzz) Time* doesn't review shows that have already closed.

PETER: We haven't closed!

JAMES: *Newsweek* left after the first act. *New York* left during the first act.

PETER: Get Brendan Gill in *The New Yorker*. He's always been a big fan of mine.

JAMES: He's coming the second night, if there is one. *(They all look at Julia. She shakes her head and weeps)* Should we cancel the blimp? *(Julia sobs)* I guess that's the ball game, Buzz.

JULIA: Tell him I'm very disappointed in his services.

JAMES: *(Hanging up)* He just told me he quit.

PETER: I wish I were dead.

JULIA: Gus, I want you to go downstairs and ask everyone to leave. Tell them the party's over.

GUS: Okay. I'll tell most of 'em, but I ain't telling that Bacall woman nothing. For what it's worth, you people: I'm sorry.

JULIA: Thank you.

GUS: It was just getting to be my turn to sing. *(He goes)*

PETER: I'll tell you one thing, Mr. Drew. God punishes people who get their plays done on Broadway. He punishes them good.

IRA: That's why He invented regional theater.

PETER: Don't give me regional theater. I'll tell you what regional theater is: plays that couldn't get produced in New York with actors who couldn't get a job in New York performed for audiences who wish they still lived in New York. This is my regional theater. Right here.

JULIA: Peter!

PETER: I still wish I was dead.

EMMA: I just hope all you nice people have the good sense not to brood over this, and get on with the next one. You heard him: onwards and upwards.

JULIA: Thank you, Emma.

EMMA: See, if this was nuclear physics I'd keep my big mouth shut, but I know something about show business. The original Harvey was a giraffe. Making him a rabbit happened in my cab.

JULIA: I can't deal with a remark like that.

JAMES: When I'd get discouraged, my father used to say, "It's only a play, Jimbo, it's only a play." Only, he said it in Italian. *"Non c'e che una commedia, Jimbo, c'e che una commedia."* He never saw me make it.

JULIA: Mine used to say, "It's only money, angel. Your money. And don't you forget it."

(Gus returns)

GUS: It's breaking up down there. I didn't have to ask. Everybody's real disappointed. The cast was wondering if there's going to be a second night.

JULIA: That's up to Peter.

PETER: What'd be the point? *(He turns away)*

GUS: They said to thank you for being the nicest producer they've ever worked with. *(He gathers more coats to take down and goes. The phone has started to ring. No one has the heart to answer it this time. Finally, Emma picks it up)*

PETER: No more calls.

EMMA: Hello? *(To Peter)* It's for you.

101

PETER: Who is it?

EMMA: Steubenville, Ohio.

(Peter walks to the phone. It is the longest mile)

PETER: Hi, Dad. How are you feeling? . . . Hi, Mom . . .
Pretty good. Not great but . . . No, not as good as *Flashes.*
Listen, can I get back to you when we have all the reviews? I
don't want to tie this— . . . I love you, too. *(He hangs up. He
is crying. A wild howl escapes him. He breaks down)*

FRANK: Hey, c'mon, man, don't. I hate emotion. *(This time, he
has heard himself)* I mean—! Wow!

(Now it is Julia who breaks down and sobs)

JULIA: It's all my fault. That turntable did matter. I'll never
forgive myself.

*(The tears are contagious. Now it is Virginia who breaks down
and sobs)*

VIRGINIA: It's my fault. I wore out my fucking welcome. I
dropped the fucking bottle, it didn't slip.

JAMES: He's right. The play never had a chance without me. I
would have been marvelous.

PETER: It's all my fault. I wrote it. Will any of you ever forgive
me?

FRANK: Hey, c'mon, you people. It's only a play. We did our
best. Oh shit, this is worse than Yale!

*(He, too, breaks down and cries and joins the others in a tearful
huddle of mutual comforting and stroking)*

EMMA: Papa! *(She, too, has broken down)* He wanted to see Finland before he died. Was that asking so very much?

(The others open their arms to her. The stage is awash in tears, real tears. Even Torch joins in with a heartrending whine from the bathroom)

JULIA: Torch!

(Gus has returned for more coats. Instead, he breaks down when he sees the wailing group and joins them, sobbing his heart out)

JULIA: It wasn't your fault, Gus.

GUS: I know.

JULIA: Then why are you crying?

GUS: I'm a nice person.

JAMES: *(To the others)* A play of Peter's did make me a star. I've never been able to admit that.

PETER: James could have saved my ass tonight. Like he did in *Flashes.* I've never been able to admit that.

JAMES: Here's to our next one.

PETER: After tonight, who'd want to produce it?

JULIA: I certainly would. Why do you think I produced this one?

PETER: I don't know. A tax loss?

JULIA: Peter!

PETER: You really liked it?

103

JULIA: And I thought a lot of other people would too. Well, I was wrong. Of course there were things wrong with your play. I wish I could have helped you fix them. I wish I had your genius for the moments that did work. We just didn't have quite enough of them. But the ones we did have were splendid. The sight of Virginia in the last act: the way that Frank had her standing, her hair, the costume, the lighting, your beautiful words . . . you could hear a pin drop.

(We see Frank "frame" Virginia with his hands as if he were directing the moment Julia is describing)

VIRGINIA: "I would dream of Persia and flying carpets and every far-off place I'd ever read of. I could dream of them under my quilt with the calico patches."

EMMA: Sounds like I missed something.

JULIA: You did, Emma. And I produced it. Anyone can come up with a tax loss. It takes a very special maniac to produce a play.

(There is a final cadenza of tears and sniffles from the surrogate "family" on the sofa. Only Ira has been excluded from this grouping)

IRA: I just don't understand you people. One minute you're at each other's throats, the next you're sticking up for one another like you're in some kind of club.

JAMES: We are.

IRA: I'm in the theater, too, you know.

VIRGINIA: On the outside looking in, baby, on the outside looking in.

IRA: I'm sorry, but I feel in.

ALL: You ain't.

(And now it is Ira's turn to break down and sob. At once, he is the center of their attention as their cares and woes are temporarily forgotten)

IRA: I can't live with it anymore! I've got to tell someone. I am Caroline Comstock.

VIRGINIA: Who?

IRA: My nom de plume. I didn't want to unduly influence anyone because of my position as a critic. I won't call *Bluestocking* a masterpiece. Let's just say it's the best American play in years. On top of everything else, it only has one set and two characters.

JULIA: You already mentioned that.

IRA: In this day and age, it bears repeating. I felt such a pang of envy when that curtain rose this evening. It's as if that set had been designed for *Bluestocking*.

PETER: They all want to be playwrights. It's a noble profession. Well, dream on, Mr. Drew. I'm not anymore.

JULIA: Don't say that.

PETER: I wrote my first play in high school. The life of George Gershwin. I got all my information from the back of record jackets. In the first scene, young George got thrown out of a music publisher's office. The secretary consoled him and shyly confessed she was a budding lyricist. "What's your name?" George asked her. "Ira," my first heroine said. I think my career has been downhill ever since. I love you all very much, I'm taking the next plane to California and where do we go from here?

EMMA: The Brasserie's open all night.

105

PETER: The salt of the earth is finally making sense. You're on and it's on me.

GUS: I'd better get the rest of these coats downstairs. *(Gus exits)*

JULIA: The thought of that beautiful theater dark even one night, or a pornographic film place, or worse, demolished!

VIRGINIA: You've offered *Bluestocking* to Meryl What's-Her-Name, right?

IRA: Meryl Streep for *Bluestocking!* Don't make me laugh.

(But we can see that the idea has enormous appeal for him)

JAMES: Who's it for? Two men, I guess? More gay theater.

IRA: It's for one man, one woman. Both fiercely heterosexual.

JULIA: Elliott would like that. He's bullish in that department.

IRA: Actually, Miss Noyes, you'd be wonderful for the role of Cubby.

VIRGINIA: Who?

IRA: Cubby. Cubby Blunt. She's sort of an Everywoman figure. Down to earth, basic, warm, very vital.

PETER: Ginny? Frank? Julia? Let's go. James?

JAMES: What about the man's role?

IRA: His name is Fred Brown.

JAMES: Fred Brown.

IRA: But that could be changed. Along with the title.

EMMA: Now you're talking. I hate *Bluestocking*. How about *Clap of Doom?* I've always thought that would make a great title for something. *Clap of Doom. (She will leave Peter to join the others over by Ira)*

IRA: Actually, George is sort of an Everyman figure, too.

JAMES: Who's George?

IRA: Fred is. I just changed it.

VIRGINIA: I thought I was the Everyman figure in this play.

IRA: You both are. George, or maybe it's Fred, after all, Fred is good, it's strong.

JAMES: I like Tucker.

IRA: Tucker is marvelous. Anyway, Tucker, Fred is down to earth, great humor, lots of warmth.

JULIA: Just like you, James.

JAMES: Virile?

IRA: Extremely. You'd be perfect for it.

JULIA: You say *Bluestocking* could be done on Peter's disk?

PETER: Julia!

JULIA: I just wondered.

IRA: With only the slightest modification.

FRANK: You mind if I take a look at this?

(He will take the script of Bluestocking *and study it)*

VIRGINIA: Can you imagine me going from one play right into another? There must be a name for something like that.

IRA: *Coup du théâtre.*

VIRGINIA: *Coup du* fucking fabulous.

JAMES: What about me going from a canceled series right into the lead of a Broadway show? There must be a name for something like that, too.

PETER: What do you people think you're doing?

JAMES: *(His bubble burst)* He's right. You'd think we were doing this *Bluestocking.* Sorry to get your hopes up.

FRANK: *(Suddenly)* He's right! It could be done on our set.

JULIA: But the Shuberts will want us out of there long before we could be ready to open this one.

FRANK: Wrong again. We could preview tomorrow.

VIRGINIA: Tomorrow? You know me and lines, Frank.

FRANK: Dig this for a concept: two actors, a bare disk.

JULIA: I'm getting goose bumps. Go on.

FRANK: That's it.

JULIA: I like it.

FRANK: Somebody . . .

(Gus enters)

GUS: That's it.

108

FRANK: —a black mute—puts a script in their hands and pushes them on. Instant theater.

VIRGINIA: I buy it.

JAMES: I love it.

JULIA: It's brilliant, Frank. What do you think, Emma?

EMMA: It sounds interesting.

IRA: But that's exactly the idea behind *Bluestocking*. The play is set in a rehearsal situation. The two actors are meant to be carrying their scripts. It's part of my concept.

FRANK: Your concept? Who's directing this show anyway? Let him direct it for you, Julia.

JULIA: Mr. Drew didn't mean it like that. Frank, we could preview tomorrow, you say?

FRANK: Preview?! We could open. No rehearsals, no rewrites, no previews. *(There is a great renewal of the spirit)* The whole risk with a project like this, Julia, is the actors getting stale.

JAMES: I don't get stale. I ripen.

PETER: What the hell is going on here?

GUS: Don't say nothing, but I think we're doing another play.

JULIA: All I'm thinking, Peter, is that with *Bluestocking*, Virginia, Frank and now James will be right back to work, Gus will get to Broadway, and the Ethel Barrymore will be blazing anew with us tomorrow night at eight.

FRANK: We need more scripts.

IRA: They're right downstairs. *(He dashes out of the room)*

109

JULIA: That reminds me, Gus, there should be a new script down there. It was just bicycled over.

GUS: Okay, but that's it. I'm in rehearsal. *(He goes)*

PETER: What do you think you're doing?

JULIA: Oh, pshaw, Peter. If you had something ready, we'd be doing yours.

PETER: Plays don't pop up like toast.

JULIA: They should! Next time, I think you should write a love story.

PETER: This one was a love story, only nobody noticed. James?

JAMES: You know there's no one I'd rather do than you.

PETER: Then don't do this to me.

JAMES: It's only a play.

PETER: Somebody else's play.

JAMES: You can't write every play.

PETER: I can want to. Virginia . . . ?

VIRGINIA: The sooner you get back up on that high wire, Peter, the better.

(Ira returns with a briefcase full of scripts)

IRA: Sorry I took so long.

PETER: You're too late. She's doing Hugh Golden.

JAMES: I have a hunch about this script!

VIRGINIA: I want a phone in my dressing room, Julia.

EMMA: *(Who has answered the phone)* The Shubert Organization again. They have to know.

JULIA: Put them on hold, Emma. James . . . ?

JAMES: I'm in.

JULIA: Virginia?

VIRGINIA: Me, too.

JULIA: Frank? Frank? Frank!

FRANK: I am in rehearsal, Julia!

JULIA: Hello, Bernie. Tell your *Leather Maidens* they can't have the Barrymore. We're staying. We're holding back the night. We're putting our fingers in the dike. Budder's back in business. *(She hangs up)*

EMMA: *(Holding out another phone)* It's your press agent.

JULIA: He quit.

EMMA: He hears you're producing a new play.

VIRGINIA: Over my dead body.

JULIA: Mine, too, Virginia. *(Into phone)* Buzz off, you asshole. *(She slams the phone down)* Now let's get crackin'.

(Gus returns with a script for Julia)

GUS: What did I miss?

PETER: Frank changed his concept. He's going with Whoopi Goldberg.

111

GUS: No fair. She's already been to Broadway.

VIRGINIA: I'm going to wear my hair in tight little curls.

JAMES: I see this guy in a plaid jumpsuit.

EMMA: Hey, you got a thunderstorm here.

IRA: I know that!

EMMA: That's something people go for in a play: special effects.

IRA: There's a typhoon in the second act.

EMMA: I'll tell you something else they go for: intermissions.

JULIA: *(Clutching the script to her bosom) Little Epiphanies* by Hubert A. Golden III. I am the luckiest woman in the world!

IRA: You're not going to read Mr. Golden's play tonight?

JULIA: You playwrights are all alike. A producer even looks at another script and you feel abandoned.

FRANK: People, we have an opening. Can we get started?

VIRGINIA: In front of him?

IRA: I don't mind.

VIRGINIA: You will.

JULIA: This is exciting.

IRA: Too exciting. I'm going to throw up.

JULIA: Nonsense. Now come and sit here by me. *(To Gus)* Congratulations, Gus.

112

GUS: *(Looking at his script)* When do I come in?

JAMES: What did I miss? I was counting my lines.

PETER: I thought you all loved me.

JULIA: We do, darling, we just love the theater more.

FRANK: *"Bluestocking,* a new play in four acts by Caroline Comstock."

IRA: Do you know how long I've waited to hear that? Eleven years.

JULIA: That's the second-saddest thing I've ever heard.

PETER: Mr. Drew?

IRA: Please, we're working.

PETER: Good luck.

FRANK: "At rise, nothing." *(To cast)* Let's make that something.

IRA: But—! It has to be nothing . . .

FRANK: If he keeps this up, I'm gonna want him barred, Julia.

EMMA: I thought of something else people want in a play. Life! Lots and lots of life.

PETER: Thanks, I'll try to remember that.

FRANK: What do all these dots mean?

IRA: Hesitations, pauses.

JAMES: I don't do hesitations.

IRA: Pinter uses dots.

FRANK: Fuck Pinter. *(He rips pages from Ira's script. James, Virginia and Gus follow suit. Ira agonizes)*

JULIA: I hope you're taking this all in, Emma. It's the real thing.

EMMA: I never knew it was like this.

JULIA: Wait! It gets better.

PETER: *(He sees his next marquee)* "*It's Only a Play*, a new play by Peter Austin."

FRANK: Lights up. "A woman screams in the distance." *(Virginia screams)* "Or is it a woman?" "Or is it a woman?" *(James screams)* "An ineffable sound."

GUS: Me?

FRANK: No, Julia. *(Julia screams)* Yes, you! *(Gus screams. A star is born)* Where have you been all my life? *(He gives Gus a big kiss)*

VIRGINIA: *(To James, low)* We got our hands full with this one.

EMMA: *(To Julia)* The kid's good.

GUS: Thank you.

FRANK: May we continue? Virginia, you'll be downstage right in a spot. James, downstage left.

(The lights begin to fade on the grouping as they continue to rehearse)

PETER: *(Beginning to create)* "The curtain rises. An opening-night party is in progress." *(The lights are beginning to fade on him, too)*

114

THE LIGHTS FADE TO BLACK

THE PLAY IS OVER

(IMPORTANT NOTE: The first curtain call is taken by Torch. He comes out of the bathroom. He is an adorable beagle)

115